Anna St. Onge

Convent Girl

Life growing up in Canadian convents

Dedication

This book is for the great love of my life, my daughter Mara, who lived a different version of a Convent Girl life through her childhood "on the Lights."

Memories in vignettes

I've never met anyone with a childhood remotely like mine — a four-year-old losing her family and, after a year in foster care, being raised by nuns until the age of 19 in a half dozen Manitoba convents.

For years, whenever I talked to people about it, they would invariably say, "That's amazing, you should write your story." Each time I resolved to do so.

This is not a formal autobiography as much as a collection of vignettes, my memories of growing up.

These writings are about how convent life shaped a naïve young girl. They testify to the life of this girl, who felt alone in each convent. These pages honour and give dignity to the child I was.

1

Our family dissolves

My mother, Thérèse St. Onge, was exceedingly religious. As a girl, she had been indoctrinated in an extreme approach to Catholicism and — even as a young mother in the early 1940s — followed a strict, self-imposed regimen of worship and devotion.

Thérèse strove to be a saint and to make saints of her two children. She liked the idea of my brother Léon and I lying in mangers like the Christ child. So we slept in specially-made nativity-style canvas beds supported by wooden crosses at both ends.

My parents, both unilingual French speakers, lived not far from the land of Gabrielle Roy's *Where Nests the Water Hen*. Arid and alkali, the infertile soil meant no more than cattle ranching was possible. Many poor families like mine survived by raising some cattle and using manure to create top-soil for a garden. Several men including my father ran trap lines, mainly for saleable muskrat pelts. Our land was a distance from the mainly French Canadian hamlet of Toutes-Aides, on the western shore of Lake Manitoba and near Spence Lake, which today is swampland.

When I was two, a fire destroyed our farmhouse and all of the family's belongings. I was alone in the house in my crib, and my mother saved me from the flames. However the stress of the fire and the increased poverty that followed took a lasting toll on her. This was compounded by the hard-scrabble, pioneer life in the Manitoba backwoods.

My mother stepped up her religious devotions, and became increasingly unstable. I remember times when she made Léon and me kneel in the attic, our arms tied for long periods in a position of prayer.

My mother eventually went quite mad and was taken to a mental hospital. I tell more of my mother's story in the section about my family.

My mother escapes us

Something big was up, but I couldn't understand what it was. I was four, and now retain only fragments, vivid shards of memory of the day they came for my mother.

I'm sitting in a corner of the attic room, hugging my knees and watching. As if she were alone, my mother fixes her hair in front of a small mirror. Looking eager and happy, she wears her finest dress, a dark taffeta with a flared skirt.

That day in the attic, I see in my mother, a new lightness of being that I could not understand. She looks hopeful and happy. I didn't know then that she was going to a new home.

Some impressive and importantly dressed men wait downstairs, clearly not the farmers we usually see. Then we are all in a car, and my mother asks to stop at the church to see the priest. Afterward, she is transferred to another vehicle that takes her away.

At the time, it seemed to me that my mother looked forward to whatever would happen. Much later in life, my brother, Léon, told me about the wrenching feeling he had when she rode away in the second car.

No choice but foster care

Keeping the St. Onge family together would not have been possible for my father, Thomas.

At the time, in isolated villages like ours, no father raised young children single-handedly. As well as the deep social resistance to fathers taking care of young children, Thomas wore exceedingly thick glasses and was legally blind.

Léon and I were placed with a local foster family.

Being a girl in a new large family seemed the best thing ever to me. I remember the following seasons on my foster family's farm, and the kind, gentle and soft-spoken mother.

For Easter, she made two identical buttercup-coloured tulle dresses for me and her own young daughter. I was bewitched by the magnificent starched dress, with fine raised dots on a yellow field and its gorgeous little flared skirt.

My brother remembers that it was my mother's wish that I be sent to the convent. In that tiny Catholic village, convent boarding school was a desirable and privileged opportunity few could afford. By then, my father received a government pension through the Canadian National Institute for the Blind, and this included provision for children in care.

After a year, I became a convent girl at the age of five. My brother remained in foster care with various families for the next five years. I didn't see him again until I was ten, during my first summer visit to the one room cabin he eventually shared with my father.

School is where I want to be

Before I moved from foster care to convent life, everyone must have told me how wonderful that life would be. I was eager and hopeful, full of thoughts about amazing possibilities.

I have a strong memory of sitting in the back of a pick-up truck, being driven to my first convent. Looking forward to an enchanted, fairytale world, I was over the moon.

At last, I would go to school, something I had always envied my brother being able to do simply because he was two years older. I remember when we were still at home, trying to follow Léon to school. He left me behind at the fence line as he crossed the ditch and took the main road.

More than anything, going to the convent felt like a truly new beginning. I am sent away, independent in life, and this is so exciting!

2

Glimpses of convent life

Rules rule, for better or worse

As a child, the word "survivor" conjured up images of a drowning person clinging desperately to a floating log. I wanted to be more than a girl just keeping her head above water.

I decided by Grade 2 that drawing conclusions and then making rules to live by would help me get through. That's when I started my mental handbook.

Feeling alone in the universe, I used this book of rules to run lines out to solid things. I liked certainties that helped me to feel stable and in control of what often felt like free fall.

My rules served me well in some ways as a child, and sometimes poorly later as an adult.

"Weren't the nuns mean and horrible?"

My convent life was not a little girl's version of *Oliver Twist*. A few nuns were mean, but only some of the time; by and large, I didn't experience abuse. I was mostly able to focus on the nuns I was attracted to.

Landing in convent life, and seeing the vast halls and endless staircases, seemed a huge improvement from the poverty of my village. I appreciated the order and cleanliness. I was really impressed with the dormitories and tidy little beds. I admired the rows of desks, the array of coat hangers, the line of sinks with running water, the long tables in the refectory.

In any case, I felt that any punishments I received were deserved. I already had a deep sense of being a difficult child, a real handful. I believed that stepping over the line meant I would be sent away, in the worst-case scenario to live with my father in the backwoods or to a "reform school."

The girls who hated the convent either came from caring, sometimes pampering families, or they had been sent there to be straightened out. Homesick, they cried every night after arriving. They complained bitterly about the food, the deprivation, the supervision, the rules and the "jail-like" atmosphere. I thought they were silly and spoiled.

Helen Colgan gives a good example of unhappiness and bitterness about convent life in her memoir *Two Girls From the Bay*. The author and her sister were placed in a Newfoundland convent after their devoted mother's sudden death broke up a warm and happy family. Older than I was, they really knew what they were missing. Both sisters found convent life a harsh and miserable existence. They had been close to their mother, whereas in my case the bond had been broken long ago.

Looking back decades later, I see clearly the neglect that I experienced in my convent upbringing. The regimented environment meant lack of tender attention, love, commitment and devoted motherly care. This created a void that I struggled to fill, not only in childhood, but also as an adult.

Years later, this all came back to me as I watched my own daughter being a mother to her children from breastfeeding to school years — attending to them, caressing and cuddling them, guiding them through the minutiae of growing up.

Her daily motherly attentions continue today, leaving me with mixed feelings of awe and admiration, sadness and loss.

Little orphan Anna

Although not an orphan, I did want to be one because of the status and simplicity of it. Being an orphan seemed easier to explain than my real situation.

To my young mind, dead parents seemed romantic, and orphans seemed unique. In my world of convent girls living ordered lives in identical school uniforms, unique felt desirable. If not different, I thought, I might easily disappear. That was one of my first rules for myself: "Don't go with the crowd; try to stand out."

I did miss having conventional, well-dressed parents to show off on visitors' day. My father's options were very limited. He lived in the bush, far away from the nearest neighbour with only a horse and buggy for transportation. He might catch a ride to the convent once a year. Still, he couldn't be considered desirably conventional, either in manner or attire.

From the outset, my father had told the nuns that I was completely in their care. I belonged to them. He had nowhere for me to stay, even on holidays. All he could do was pay for my convent upbringing with his meagre pension. Mother Superior would make all the decisions about how I would be raised.

Of all the girls in all my convents over the years, only I "belonged to the nuns." I was the single boarder living full-time with the sisters and staying in the convent when my classmates went home on holidays.

I cultivated my unique status. Most girls tried to fit in, but I wanted to be different. In Grade 9, a teaching nun stressed that we should write original essays instead of copying ideas from books. One girl asked, "Who is the most original girl here?" When the nun instantly pointed to me, I glowed with pride. Throughout childhood, I was an attention seeker and loved standing out.

When I was five or six, some older girls also gave me unusually special attention. They stood me at the end of a hall, out of the nuns' hearing, and encouraged me to chant a lilting ditty: *"I am a little orphan/my mommy she is dead/my daddy isn't with me/and I am here instead."* I made up lines as I went along.

The older girls also told one another not to pay too much attention to me because "she can be a pest."

So I did become an orphan in a way. Being a pretty orphan, however, would have been infinitely better.

Where is my cuteness factor?

Some other convent girls were cute. The first I remember noticing this was in Grade 1. Yvette's shiny hair fell in golden ringlets, framed by carefully-placed ribbons. Her family was prominent in the village, and she was chosen to be Mary in the Christmas pageant.

On Saturday nights at St. Eustache, my second convent, the nuns occasionally fixed my hair as Yvette's had been done — pulled tight and wound in long strips of cloth. So I had ringlets in well-placed ribbons for Mass on Sunday mornings, and this helped somewhat for a time.

All the while, the nuns conveyed to me, both subtly and sometimes overtly, that focusing on one's appearance was vain, shallow, impious and somehow connected to boy craziness. The sisters also made sensible choices for me: plain haircuts, and carefully-sized Buster Brown shoes. I particularly remember the fuss made over my shoes. At that time, this qualified as sound parental care.

Unfortunately, no one paid much attention to the state of my underclothes. In the early years, I constantly had to pull up bloomers several sizes too big. Defective garter belts meant I was constantly hoisting falling lisle cotton stockings. I finally managed to hold them in place by using tightly-stretched sealer jar rings as garters.

When not pretending to lose my hated pink plastic glasses, I wriggled my nose a lot to keep them from slipping off my head. A "lazy eye" meant wearing an eye patch, which I managed to flush down the toilet.

Spotty personal hygiene caused rashes and chafe marks, and brushing my teeth was sometimes only an afterthought.

Later, most teen convent girls spent evenings systematically and carefully putting their hair in curlers. I did this also, but carelessly, rarely consulting the mirror; the next morning, my unruly hair always looked as if it had been through a minor windstorm.

All of this definitely lowered my cuteness factor. I needed a mom.

My mother is "dead-ish"

No one at the convent mentioned my mother, and it took me what seemed like a lifetime to ask about her. The subject felt dangerous. If it did come up, there was silence. So I invented a word to describe my mother's situation: 'dead-ish.' I never said the word for anyone to hear.

But I wondered about my mother. At eight, being the only child in the convent over the summer, I was once with a nun doing laundry in the basement. She was pulling a thick sheet through an old wringer washing machine, and I asked, "What happened to my mother?" As the sister stopped working, I thought, "Oh, no, when they take a long time to answer it's never good."

Finally, the answer came: "Your mother has a sickness ... it's in her head."

I went to the swings to think that over. Swinging higher and higher, I told myself, "My mother is cuckoo, and that is not good. I can't tell anybody about that."

After this revelation, I made up stories about my mother. For example, I told another girl that an impressive picture of a Greek goddess looked exactly like my mother.

About the same time that I learned about her "sickness," I told classmates that Mother Superior was really my aunt. This was to imply that I was connected to important people. However, the story came back to haunt me.

On Sundays, after Mass and the main meal, the convent parlour was often full of visitors for the resident girls. I rarely received visitors and was astounded one Sunday to be told that someone was in the parlour to see me.

Entering the room, I saw only strangers and some nuns. Then Mother Superior rose from a chair by the door, led me by the hand to the centre of the room and announced in a kindly voice, "This is my niece."

It never occurred to me that any of the nuns would hear the story about my "aunt." Ashamed at being caught in such a great lie, I flung up my right arm and buried my face in my elbow.

Imaginary hugs work

Years after the fact, chatting about our early teen convent life, a former class-mate surprised me by saying, "You know, the nuns didn't have an ounce of maternal instinct."

With a loving, devoted mother at home, this friend could recognize a lack that I had never seen, let alone understood while in the convent.

Quite simply, hugging wasn't part of my upbringing, although I would have liked it.

Once, when I had just arrived at my first convent, I was watching a movie with others in the common area, and Mother Superior placed me on her knee. I remember feeling awkward and uncomfortable, pleased and flattered at the same time. That was the first and last time I remember being held.

Through all the years that followed — whenever I felt humiliated, over-looked or hurt in the daily grind of convent life — I sought comfort from imaginary hugs.

Choosing a nun whose attention I would have liked, I repeated to myself again and again, "Sister Constance gave me a hug, Sister Constance gave me a hug, Sister Constance gave me a hug." This calmed and soothed me. Another rule I constructed for myself was, "If you don't have it, pretend that you do."

This really helped in the convent. But later as an adult, I might pretend somebody loved me when in fact they weren't all that interested.

I want to be classy, and red is not classy

In Grade 1, red was the most important colour in the crayon box. I didn't think it the prettiest or the best, but red seemed big as a house compared to any of the other colours.

The importance of red might go back to the memory of a pre-convent experience in a farm field. I remember my angry, frightened father scooping me up while yelling, "You never, never never wear red in front of a bull!"

I felt shocked and aggrieved. This was long before anyone recognized how very much I needed glasses. The toddler I was didn't know what colour she wore, and had not actually seen the bull.

Red was also an issue in the convent. In Grade 3, the nuns didn't let me select a piece of red clothing from the Missions hamper. They pronounced it as a distasteful colour that only "common" people wore. Thus I avoided red clothing for a long time, well into adulthood. The sisters had other ideas about bright colours worn together, which they thought denoted lack of "good breeding."

The nuns tried to instruct me in their ideas about class, frequently referring to certain people or things as vulgar, coarse, or common. I took pains to avoid being seen that way. Thus when most of the girls listened to Elvis Presley, I boasted that Beethoven and Bach were the only musicians worth listening to.

Convents, convents, convents

I never knew why Mother Superior at my very first convent, St. Rose du Lac, decided, sometime before Christmas in Grade 2, to send me off to another convent. I always believed that it was because I wasn't well behaved and that the nuns thought another smaller convent would be better for me. It could have been for any reason however. I'll just never know.

My second convent, St. Eustache, was 153 miles away and closer to Winnipeg. Then, sometime in Grade 4, the Mother Superior there decided that I should be moved again, to Grande-Clairière, 161 miles away toward Brandon.

Grande-Clairière, a tiny house convent, had only three nuns. For the first time, I felt uprooted and miserable. Everything and everybody seemed strange, shiny and unreal. I cried every day and couldn't eat, so I was sent back to St. Rose du Lac.

The next move was to Laurier, just southwest of St. Rose du Lac. This was followed by a year in St. Laurent Convent whose Franciscans served a Metis community.

My last and favourite convent was St. Charles Academy, where I spent five years before earning a high school diploma.

In addition to those all-school-year boarding convents, I spent high school summers in what I called my two "summer convents."

The boarding school convents were the essentially the same, with rules, schedules, chores, prayers, study times, mealtimes, bedtimes and classroom times.

Where they differed were the overall atmosphere and things like strictness, focus on ladylike behaviours or education. This depended on the nuns' Order or Congregation and their Mission. Other differences which had an impact were the tones of the Mother Superiors and the personalities of the influential nuns. Some convents had greater separation between teaching nuns and kitchen nuns, and more apparent class distinctions between them.

How were my convents different from residential schools for Aboriginal children? Only by degrees. The Order of Oblate nuns at St. Charles Academy, for example, also ran residential schools for students further north. Every summer, the nuns were told if they would be assigned to a residential school or a southern convent with fewer Aboriginal students.

In every convent where I lived, there were always some First Nations kids who attended, some more willingly than others. However, they were not singled out since most were Métis, and many of the French Canadian students had some Métis in their ancestry.

Just as today, non-Aboriginal Manitobans had negative stereotypes about native people. Within the convent walls we felt those negative stereotypes. However, I didn't recognize any active discrimination; but early on, I remember thanking God I hadn't been born a First Nations girl.

Books launch you out of this world

In Grade 2, I discovered fairytales. I loved them, especially if they had pictures. I scoured the library for them.

Fairytales were only the beginning. For the rest of my childhood, I always had a book to escape into.

I could count on books to stave off boredom (convents are profoundly boring). Books also helped me deal with rejection, loneliness, humiliation and other unpleasant emotions and situations.

I read everywhere — on the playground and in the recreation room surrounded by screaming children. I read sitting in stairwells and under stairs, in quiet hidden corners, and empty classrooms, even waiting in lines, and in the refectory wolfing down nondescript food. There were always books secreted on my knees below the cover of the desks.

Most books donated to the convent libraries were in English, the language of all convent teaching except for time-limited French classes.

Initially, most library books were English and Victorian classics, although the high school library later offered a wider range of subjects: Catherine the Great, Napoleon, Alexander the Great, the Ptolemys and other royals. Their stories featured lurid and vivid depictions of family members scheming and murdering one another in various horrific ways. Thus I felt more informed about the world outside convents.

Still, I loved the classics and their lofty ideas about romantic love and women's role in society. I wanted to emulate the qualities of my Jane Austen heroines — to be "reserved," "composed," "thoughtful" and "good." Given my extroverted and outspoken personality, this was an arduous struggle, regularly undertaken.

I loved and identified with Anne of Green Gables (imaginative and impulsively spontaneous) and Jane Eyre (quiet, yet forthright, standing in the background and maintaining high principles). I simultaneously wanted to be both Beth and Jo from *Little Women,* one good and submissive, the other wild and adventurous.

Coming out of a book, I tried as long as possible to be its heroine. Later in life, an old and steadfast convent friend told me that during high school, my personality changed every week. I told her that I tried to change with every novel.

Escaping boredom without books

It wasn't evident to me at the time, but most of the other girls worked hard to please their parents. As for me, I couldn't make myself feel consistently interested in schoolwork. Mainly, I wasn't trying to please anyone.

Finally, about the age of eight, I hit upon the idea of having a "pretend" someone watching me from above. I would pick a nun I liked, or an imaginary person who adored me, or a Greek or Roman goddess I admired. I pictured her paying close attention to me — for instance, as I carefully polished my handwriting. This pretend figure was always a woman, and invariably impressed with everything I did.

Sustaining this was difficult after a short while, and I would eventually lapse into my default comfort zone: reading books.

In some places, however, books couldn't be used to escape the mind-numbing boredom. I would turn then to the pleasures of daydreaming.

One example was in chapel, where we went at least twice a day, for morning Mass and later the Rosary. My system was to offer a few moments of devout prayer, especially when the liturgy was most dramatic. This reassured me that I was not a bad girl. It required only a bit of intense invocation along the lines of: "Dear God, please, please, please help me be a good girl." After paying my respects to the forces of good, I would launch into my favourite daydreams.

One scenario that I used for years was to imagine being shipwrecked on a desert island with only one or two tools (my homage to *Robinson Crusoe*). Most of my endeavours centred on making shelter. Start with the floor? Use rushes or ferns? How can I construct the roof, and make it leak-proof? As I worked out the details, time passed quickly — in chapel or anywhere else I wanted to escape from.

The classroom was one place where escapist reading could be difficult. It wasn't always possible to sneak a book under the corner of my desk, and daydreaming here was less structured. I stared fixedly at the teacher with what I supposed was an intelligent expression, and entertained myself with fleeting scenarios based on the topic of study.

Of course, I always performed brilliantly in my daydreams.

Be smart if you can't be beautiful

When reading fairytales, I noted with satisfaction that princesses never failed to be beautiful. In fact, "beautiful princess" went together like "bread and butter" or "horse and carriage."

It would have disturbed me if a princess were plain or ugly. Those words described people like step sisters, villains and minor characters in the fairytale.

Once when I was about seven, during a holiday when all the other resident girls were gone, the nuns did a major cleaning of the convent. Part of this undertaking was removing all the pictures and mirrors and putting them face-up on counters, tables and other horizontal surfaces.

This offered me a different vantage point, a novel and more objective view of my face in a mirror. Looking down, it didn't take long for me to recognize that I wasn't very pretty. I could see from my long face and prominent nose that I wouldn't grow up to be a beautiful princess.

I remember the room I was in, the table where the mirror lay and the direction I faced. Backing up in dismay, I made a firm resolution then and there that I never forgot. "I am going to have to be smart," I told myself.

From that day on, I took bigger books from the library, tomes with little or no pictures, and I struggled through denser content. My efforts were rewarded one day when I heard one nun whisper to another, "See how smart she is, able to read those big books."

I was on my way.

That fairytale feeling

For a long time, I didn't know that I had a birthday, and assumed birthdays belonged only to children with families. The nuns would ask when my birthday was, and I informed them that I didn't have one.

That ended when the nuns of St. Eustache, my second convent, prepared for my confirmation. They ordered my baptismal certificate from my home village of Toutes-Aides, and this showed that I was a year younger than previously thought. It also prompted a huge, formal surprise party for my eighth birthday.

Ushered into the dining hall, I found a table draped with white tablecloths and the entire convent waiting to see my reaction to the cake and presents. (This explained an earlier puzzling question from the cook about my preference for vanilla or chocolate.)

I felt compelled to crow with delight and appreciation. I received my first doll then, and she bleated "mama" when laid on her back.

The party is linked in my mind to a separate event in the same year, but a world away from mine. The coronation of Queen Elizabeth II was a big day in my memory, an actual princess crowned a real queen!

Like my first birthday party, the coronation seemed magical. It represented the fairytale, make-believe world that I had hoped for while riding in the pick-up truck to my first convent.

A place to belong

I felt at home with the nuns at St. Eustache convent because they tried to make me feel that little orphan Anna belonged especially to them.

The nuns had a handsome tunic custom-made for me to wear that first Christmas. It was green and sported a myriad of pretty metallic buttons. One nun in particular made it her job to regularly search the Missions' hampers to find pretty hand-me-down blouses for me to wear when the convent uniform wasn't required.

Still, I had lonely times during the summers, hearing the nuns laughing and talking in their cloistered refectory and recreation hall which were out of bounds to me.

The cook understood this and before joining the other nuns, would prepare me a carefully arranged dinner in the kitchen with far too much food. (I felt I should eat everything to show appreciation, which started my life-long journey of eating for comfort).

When the nuns chanted afternoon vespers in the chapel, I stayed close under the stained glass windows. I felt a rhythmic peacefulness going back and forth on the sidewalk, with one knee in a little red wagon that I pushed with the other leg.

I spent a great deal of time reading under the trees in the verdant convent garden, and after lunch napped in the dormitory. A few times, I woke to the sound of a downpour outside, and realized to my horror that I had forgotten some books that became soaked in the garden.

Once, a fair came to town and set up just across the street. Excited for me about the good time I might have, the nuns gave me money for rides. I carried their anticipation with me, holding the coins tightly in my hand. But some village children wheedled all the money away from me, and I could do none of what the nuns had imagined. Afterward, I felt wretched, lying to them about how much fun the fair had been.

I remember creating a secret hideaway in the hidden recesses under a veranda, and playing house with my doll propped on a box. I made a little kitchen with a board on top of two barrels, jars and cans for dinnerware, and a pan for a sink. I even hit on an ingenious idea for a bathroom, using a bucket to pee in so that I could avoid running inside and down the long convent halls to relieve myself.

My hideaway brought happy days, playing house and washing make-believe dishes just like the kitchen nuns. One day, my secret was discovered by a nun who went almost apoplectic about the pee-filled bucket. She made me empty it in the back garden, and I felt suitably chastened and ashamed.

I am not certain whether or not that bucket of pee was the reason, but I was moved to another convent at the beginning of Grade 4.

If you want to relax, get a housecoat

In all my convents, Saturdays were relaxed times. Nice things happened then, such as housecoats, which we called kimonos. They were a big thing for us convent girls.

Housecoats signalled that rules were relaxed. We could hang around the dormitories in our voluminous kimonos while we took turns bathing (no showers in the dorms, just a couple of cubicles with individual bathtubs).

Later, at my last convent, senior girls in Grades 11 and 12 graduated from dorms to the wonders of Nazareth. This was a big, comfortable old four-story mansion just across the street from the main convent grounds. There, two or three girls shared a room, with senior girls having only one room-mate each.

Saturday nights in Nazareth meant wandering around after supper in our housecoats — showering or taking baths, curling our hair and visiting while listening to hit parade songs on the radio.

Before bed, we went to the kitchen and had toast with jam, peanut butter or lemon butter… which I loved! A couple of nuns shared the big table with us, and they were usually jolly and relaxed during that time.

Don't sew, you're no good at it

Saturdays weren't all fun and housecoats; they were also when we had to mend our cotton lisle stockings. The toes and heels wore out a lot, and throwing them away just would not do.

The nuns had nifty little wood "darning mushrooms" which we could borrow if we asked nicely (actually, begged). When mushrooms weren't available, we put light bulbs into the stockings to support our tortuous sewing efforts.

My problem was somehow always losing the previous week's needle and spending a good part of the darning session searching for the proverbial needle in a convent.

But lack of a needle didn't excuse me from the sewing ordeal. I received a replacement needle, with serious admonishments about not losing it again. Then began my attempts to weave strands of thread to cover the hole in my stocking. It wasn't unusual for the nun in charge to look aghast at my unshapely work, scissor it out completely, and tell me to start over.

A vivid memory of St. Eustache is when, as an eight-year-old, I had lost my needle again and bent over the stairs trying to find it, not an easy task because I was crying so hard. A nun had ordered me to search for that needle until I found it, and another sister confronted the first one at the top of the stairs. I overheard their exchange, and was eventually freed to join the other girls.

I was both flummoxed and grateful. It was the first and only time in my convent experience that I overheard two nuns disagree about how I should be treated. This was novel in two ways: I had never before heard the sisters disagree, and certainly never heard a front-line nun stick up for me.

My competing, parallel universes

Growing up, I learned almost unconsciously to maintain competing beliefs and feelings about very basic facets of life. I was quite comfortable running dual, incompatible realities in my imagination. Compartmentalization started early and became second nature.

As a five-year-old French speaker, I was astonished to learn that one item could have different names. "Stove" is the first English word I remember hearing, and I asked all kinds of questions about the names of other objects in this new language.

Gender also played a part in how the world was divided. In my mind, French was the girl part of life and English the boy side. I thought horses and dogs were in the boy category, while cows and cats were girls. Bulls were scary monsters in a special category all their own. When I heard about other languages like Spanish, I thought each had a French girl part and an English boy part.

Later, we learned different Canadian histories in our French and English classes. There seemed to be two countries, both called Canada.

In Grade 4 science, I realized that the existence of God was probably a fabrication. How could God manage to keep up with billions of galaxies and stars and planets? Still, I kept Him (yes, capitalized) in another compartment of my brain as a much needed person to confide in. During my teens, I managed to feel simultaneously pious and agnostic.

As well, I could feel happy and sad at virtually the same time. I ran through the convent halls, propelled by hope and general optimism, while humming sad songs to myself about loss and longing, and all the faraway places and palaces where I really belonged.

Good or bad — what shall I be?

In the convent, super heroes were saints, and we heard and read a great deal about them. All of the saints came across as really good. The nuns likewise strove to be good. I also really wanted to be good.

Being good meant being quiet, submissive, eager to follow orders and obedient in every way. It was all about trying hard to be a better person, never ceasing to improve. If one couldn't manage her behaviour, praying to be good was deemed to be helpful.

Still, I ran in the halls a lot, raced up and down stairwells three steps at a time, and became airborne swinging from one flight of stairs to the next. Occasionally, I collided with a nun.

I had a loud laugh and was noisy, disruptive, impulsive — as well as messy, forgetful and careless with my belongings and my school work.

How did it feel to be me as a child? Picture a big motor running at top speed in my chest. It kept me constantly on the move, asking questions and seeking attention. Only a book, daydreaming or a lot of food would quiet me.

When a classroom topic interested me, I couldn't stay still or listen attentively, but would interrupt the teacher and classmates with questions and comments. I often tried to grasp general ideas, and then jumped to larger concepts that caught my curiosity but weren't really the point of discussion.

I daydreamed when bored, unable to focus on work requiring attention to detail, or care, diligence and effort.

Treating the nuns like parents, I often took liberties, answering back and being sassy and mouthy. Girls with regular families didn't feel at home in the convent and weren't as brazen as I was.

Looking back decades later, I understand that what prevented me from being good was a mild form of ADHD (attention deficit hyperactivity disorder).

Looking around the convent, I saw girls who seemed saintly — naturally obedient, industrious and hardly noticeable in the classroom. I decided their way was hard, and wondered whether it was worth the struggle.

A small war raged in my heart and brain. Be good and disappear, or act up and get the attention I craved. I went back and forth, periodically praying with great intensity to be good. I admired obedience as a desirable virtue that was unattainable. It was a losing battle.

The nuns also went back and forth with me. They tried talking virtue into me: "You will never go far if you do not learn to behave." But over time, as their lectures failed to take, most of them left me to my own devices. Typically, these were daydreaming, reading and, later, playing the piano.

Running in the dark: winter

Convent corridors and stairwells usually remained unlit during the long sombre hours of a Manitoba winter. This meant dark treks for girls who forgot books or something else in another part of the convent.

But I rescued them. Quite early, I developed the skill of moving easily and quickly through the often pitch black passages. I made a name for myself as "the girl who is not afraid of the dark." I traveled the halls and stairwells at dizzying speed.

During holidays, with no other girls in the convent, I learned to run free and unnoticed through the dark. I thought nothing of moving swiftly, trailing my hands along shadowy walls and banisters, recognizing every corner, and knowing the number of steps on every staircase.

Ultimately, it became an art form for me, slipping away from places I was supposed to be — the recreation room, dining hall, the chapel. This was part of my secret life, something of my own that no one else could touch.

Running in the dark: summer

For a few relaxed teenage summers, I lived at urban "summer" convents and refined my travelling-in-the-dark skills.

One convent named L'Ecole Ménagère consisted of inter-connected buildings occupying a full city block. I lived at one end of the complex linked to a school that was empty for the summer connected to the sprawling "Mother House Convent." All this was situated in St. Boniface at the cross streets of Rue Masson and Rue Aulneau.

The basement levels were storage areas linked by arrays of staircases and short maze-like tunnels. I learned to navigate this cluttered underworld, running at high speed in the dark, reaching out with both hands, and carefully placing my running feet.

From one subterranean chamber, I could pop up minutes later anywhere else in the convent that I chose. It gave me an enormous sense of power and exhilaration.

But there were other reasons to love this convent. During the regular school year, nuns in other boarding school convents saw me as a "problem child." But at L'Ecole Ménagère in summer, I was seen as a nice girl, a young woman spending her time reading and playing the piano. I had all the freedom I craved — as long as I was helpful, showed no interest in boys, and appeared devout.

My summer convents weren't boarding schools per se. But they provided a residence for young women working in the community, many of them hospital nurses. Rural teachers taking summer courses also received room and board there.

During the school year, one summer convent offered sewing classes for girls in the community. Another one gave home economics classes for girls not deemed to be academically inclined; these were seen as potential domestic workers and stay-at-home wives.

Again, I had special status in the summer convents. I was younger than those taking classes and the only girl who lived there full time without a family to return to.

No chaos in dormitories

Convent dormitories were models of orderly, almost military "in-a-row-ness." As far as the eye could see, it was bed-dresser, bed-dresser, bed-dresser.

On each little dresser, or chiffonier, stood a basin, a pitcher and a soap dish. Every morning and evening, we took our jugs to the bathroom, filled them with tap water and went back to the dorm to wash ourselves and brush our teeth at our basins.

A girl's dresser reflected her level of neatness. Mine was a messy little wasteland.

Beds were much the same. The ideal had no lumps or wrinkles, with sheet corners squarely tucked in. If any bed wasn't perfect and identical to the others, the nuns pulled it apart for the culpable girl to remake.

If you wet the bed, a silent, grim-faced nun would strip it and march you to a big sink to scrub your sheets free of the shameful evidence.

Still, I appreciated the soldierly lines and smartness of the dormitories. They made me feel safe and clean, part of a nice and special world away from the chaotic realm of family life.

Dormitories and modesty

It might seem that girls in an open dormitory with little privacy would find nudity commonplace. But under the influence of the church and the nuns, each of us strove mightily to be scrupulous about covering up when changing clothes or climbing into pyjamas.

Dressing gowns were draped cleverly over the shoulders to swiftly manage all manner of undress with absolutely no skin exposed. Even so, the unspoken rule was to always look away when any girl arranged her clothing under a robe.

There was no mistaking the fact that modesty was a serious issue. Early on, I had to wear my undershirt and panties in the bathtub, soaping them and me thoroughly. Bathing was supervised by a nun who occasionally came into the cubicle; it couldn't be locked from the inside.

I wasn't allowed to bathe privately until I was about eight, and even older girls exercised extreme modesty.

As a young girl, I came to believe that the breasts were the centre of a woman's untouchable domain. I extrapolated from this that virginity resided there, and that the breasts were where babies came from. It was a long time before I knew otherwise.

How I come to be a dormitory delight

In Grade 3, I developed a coterie of admirers, an audience made up of the other girls in my dormitory. They crowded around my bed after the supervising nun had turned out the lights and gone away.

The attraction I had was a gift of storytelling. I would launch into a tale and make it up as I went along, never knowing where the story would go. The plot's twists and turns surprised me as much as it did the little girls who followed the story closely.

For example, I often started the story with an escaping rabbit speeding through the fields and running into all sorts of adventures and bizarre situations from which he eventually extricated himself.

I loved being the centre of attention like this.

Dormitory exile and return

When I was about twelve, I found another way to get attention — playing practical jokes on the other girls in the dormitory.

There were all sorts of tricks to play, such as sprinkling sugar liberally between the girls' bed sheets, and leaving wet facecloths under their pillows.

It was all hilarious to me, and I would laugh and laugh. One evening, however, I was shocked to find that my bed and dresser were gone! Where they had been that morning, there was an empty space.

The supervising sister showed me to my new home behind a screen at the far end of the corridor outside of the dorm. Exiled.

I understood for the first time that my practical jokes might not be so funny for the victims. I crept to my bed behind the screen and for the next month endeavoured to pretend that this new situation was normal.

After a while, however, I started to enjoy my private little alcove with its very own window.

Then, as we filed into the dorm one evening, I saw that my bed had been returned to its old location. This gave me mixed feelings of relief and mild disappointment.

Am I really cuckoo like my mother?

About the time of my practical joker's career, I started to experience bouts of insomnia, to which I responded with my usual habit of daydreaming.

One sleepless Saturday night, I tiptoed to the window at the end of the long row of dormitory beds. Gazing at the northern lights, I imagined myself as the fairytale heroine Rapunzel, shut away in a castle and communing with the stars and the flickering aurora borealis.

Then I heard a nun leave her room at the other end of the dorm, heading for the sisters' bathroom. I ducked to avoid being seen, but she passed my bed and noticed that it was empty.

It was too far to run back to bed, so I stayed in a crouch, hoping the nun would leave. Instead, she woke three other nuns in their rooms at the end of the dorm. They began searching under all the beds, advancing quickly to my hiding place.

Panicked now, I crawled along the dormitory wall and ducked behind a curtain — and into a young novice's sleeping alcove. Before I could whisper that the crouching figure at her bedside was just Anna, the novice awoke, screamed and fainted.

In stony silence, the nuns dragged me ignominiously to my bed. The other girls whispered and tried to understand what was happening. I lay awake all night, trying to imagine what punishment awaited me.

Sunday dawned, and nothing was said; nothing was done. Ominous silence prevailed. I detected, however, increasing distance and quiet watchfulness from the supervising and teaching nuns.

Not long after, Mother Superior took me to a nearby city for a full day of psychiatric evaluation. The doctors were from the Brandon mental hospital where my mother lived, and they knew her.

Ultimately, and as I found out later, the barrage of tests showed conclusively that my personality was nothing at all like my mother's. I was relieved to be certified honest, open, loyal and not devious. I was noted to be intelligent, and very inclined to literature though not at all to mathematics.

I remember several things from the tests. One was pride at knowing the capital of Greece (from having read so much mythology). I also felt silly for not knowing why oil floats on water. Thinking that oil had some magical quality, I gave a convoluted wrong answer, instead of saying correctly that it was simply the lighter liquid.

But what really stood out was a personal interview with one of the doctors. It was in the afternoon, after all the testing. He sat behind a desk in front of me, leaned forward and gently asked, "How does it feel in there... to be you?"

It was the first time I had been approached in this way. I burst into tears, sobbed uncontrollably and cried through the rest of the interview.

I just cannot win at the numbers game

Excelling in the classroom never interested me. All I wanted was to squeak by without failing. I gave myself the excuse of having had a bad start — brought to the convent a full month after the school year began, I was thought to be six when I was only five.

Most convent instruction was in English, while I only spoke French. The nun teaching Grade 1 was sweet and kind, but unprepared for a student with English as a second language.

My poor vision meant I couldn't see more than a couple of feet in front of me. No one noticed for quite a while. Not really knowing that I couldn't see, I just thought that I couldn't understand things because of the new and different language.

It was several months before I had prescription glasses. The delay was costly, especially in studying arithmetic.

Other girls shouted answers to math problems on flashcards that I could not see. Thinking the shouts indicated only the cards' sequence, I paid no attention and amused myself playing with plasticine.

A compliant, studious child might have overcome these difficulties. Feeling inherently defective, however, I did nothing to improve my work. A helpful teacher at my desk would be resisted, met by a raised shoulder, and my insistently whispered, "I know, I know."

Eventually, I was left to my own devices — daydreaming during arithmetic, and paying close attention to stories and books. I fell farther and farther behind. Once in Grade 3, I snapped out of a daydream when the teacher said, "Why, this one is so easy that even Anna would have gotten it."

Within a few years, the imbalance was pronounced. This problem with arithmetic led to repeating Grade 4.

I earned adequate grades or squeaked by in reading-based subjects like English and social studies. But I couldn't manage even basic addition because of what had become math phobia.

Any questions dealing with numbers threw me into an instant debilitating panic. Mathematics became a strange language for me, one I still have trouble with today.

Be a pest, and teachers will leave you alone

If I went underground when it came to arithmetic, I was overly involved with classes in my favourite subjects like English, history and social studies.

I asked endless questions and constantly had my hand up, demanding attention and the chance to be heard.

Without wanting to, I was a thorn in the side of the teachers. They made this very clear, consistently allowing any girl but me to answer questions, in spite of my eagerly waving hand.

Eventually, teachers looked away gratefully when I pulled out a book, any book, from my desk and ignored the class to read whatever took my fancy.

Over time, I stopped raising my hand, and didn't turn in much math homework. I was almost entirely free of classroom concerns, except for occupying a physical space.

After a few years, my copious reading served me exceedingly well in terms of other areas — comprehension of complex ideas, creativity, literature, subtle symbolism in advanced poetry, writing and other literary pursuits.

Later as a teen, I would help rural teachers taking courses in my summer convents to decipher their poetry homework and compose their essays.

Food, "glorious" food

Convent food was awful. This was the judgment of girls who could compare it to home cooking, although I didn't know any better. All of us were driven by hunger; anticipation was usually in the air as we lined up to eat, but the sameness of our meals was often disappointing.

Breakfast

The main dish alternated between puffed wheat or rice, oatmeal and Cream of Wheat. But no one starved. There were always second helpings, toast, sugar and milk aplenty.

Dinner and Supper

The day's main meal, dinner, was at midday, with supper around six. The two meals were quite similar: meat, potatoes and vegetables, often accompanied in winter by soup.

The meat was recognizable when the week started and went through daily transformations until Thursday, when shepherd's pie from leftovers was typical. Fridays, of course, brought fish.

Vegetables were generally cooked peas and carrots, creamed corn or stewed tomatoes.

Dessert was mainly rhubarb or crab apples or plums or prunes — all stewed. Occasionally, we had bread pudding or rice pudding. A favourite was blanc mange, a kind of flan.

As diners, convent girls were generally of two types: those disguising their food with ketchup, and others pouring mustard on everything. I was a mustard-and-pepper girl.

Most of us developed cast-iron stomachs, learning to eat foods like leathery liver and disgusting looking blood pudding.

We also ate fast, even when the food wasn't too bad. Why? One reason might be to get another portion of a rare tasty treat like roast chicken. Often, it was to finish as a group, wash the dishes and run outside to play before the inevitable next bell.

No one lingered at the table for civilized conversation.

Four o'clock: l'heure du goûter

Every afternoon had snack time after school and before rosary.

Girls with spending money from parents could buy chocolate bars from a cart wheeled out of a locked room by a nun. The cart was also where some lucky girls stored care packages with home-baked goodies or other booty sent by families.

Snacks for the less fortunate were usually the inevitable apple or orange. But there was always a buzz in the air in case this day might be the unusual one when convent cookies or pieces of cake were served.

Even now, I am not partial to apples or oranges and, for a long time as an adult, thought of chocolate bars as the only treats worth having.

What's in a name, in my name?

I found a special climate of camaraderie and friendliness with my Grade 6 and 7 classmates at Laurier Convent.

Several of the girls came from far-away parts of Manitoba and went home during the summer and for high holidays like Christmas and Easter. But we became close, and gave each other special nicknames that stuck. Clementine for some reason was Chinny or Chinny Chin (she and I still keep in touch). Rosalie was teasingly named Rosie Pig. Lillian, a bit heavy, was Tubby.

I was pleased to become Annabanna. I clung proudly to that nickname. I still introduce myself with it because the name makes people laugh and relaxes them. I like that.

Anna to Anne to Anna

As a child, I detested the French Canadian pronunciation of my name — especially when displeased nuns shouted it at me as "An-NUH." So at St. Laurent Convent, I became Anne (for *Anne of Green Gables* whom I loved).

Anna disappeared for a long time. For decades, I was Anne at work and with friends. Then in my forties, I became Anna again, using the English pronunciation that gives equal weight to each syllable.

The right kind of man to marry

The nuns rarely mentioned men. But when they were discussed, it was as a necessary evil described in a blend of good humour, caution and pity. The message seemed to be this.

"Poor dears, men can't help being brutish, but they are brilliant and useful in many respects. Women must defer to them because men believe they rule, and they do this with physical might. One must work to boost their egos and let them have the illusion that they are in charge.

"Women, however, are superior in important ways that really count, such as the capacity for love, and in the moral and spiritual spheres.

"One must be careful around men because they contain all that is evil in the world. It is their place to do the dirty work, the killing and the making of things."

This seemed to play out in parochial school classrooms where we sometimes studied alongside boys. Not interested in conversation, they were devoted to roughhousing, tormenting others and hunting small animals and birds.

Men on the farms that I occasionally visited were aloof, only grunting at their wives and children, and apparently uninterested in conversation and books.

Of course, nuns respected and catered to priests. In a league of their own, priests were educated, mild-mannered men, looking spiritual, thoughtful and bookish and somehow gazing at the heavens.

The lesson was clear. If I ever married, it would be to someone who was educated, could carry on a conversation and have the qualities of a priest.

Who is Mother Superior?

In each of my convents, Mother Superior was the supreme overseer of everyone and everything. She made all of the important decisions and communicated for the convent with its Mother House and the outside world.

Mother Superior typically stayed at a distance from the resident girls, and we encountered her only occasionally in hallways, at general assemblies and in chapel.

In the early 1950s, the girls were required to curtsey when meeting her. Our eyes were to be kept lowered; looking at her too long was considered insolent. This was not stated outright, just modelled by the older girls.

I was sent to Mother Superior's office when I disgraced myself, usually through disobedience or insolence. Talking back was not tolerated.

Mother Superior also sent me to spend bits of time with families in the local area, and made the decision to transfer me to another convent if she thought this beneficial. She usually dealt with my father on his yearly visits to the convent.

I remember two Mother Superiors well and with gratitude: Mother Superior Louis-Marie of Laurier Convent and, most important, Mother Superior Augustine of St. Charles Academy.

An unforgettable Mother Superior

The head of Laurier Convent, Mother Superior Louis-Marie, made a lifelong impression on me.

For instance, usually on Sundays after Mass and breakfast, she often fetched me from the dining hall or school yard or wherever I happened to be. We would go alone to the rarely-used formal "high" parlour for energized and passionate lectures. The general theme was about improving my behaviour. Individual topics ranged from obedience to ladylike comportment to the state and salvation of my soul. I never knew how to arrange my face or what to say. She seemed so ancient; it was basically one-way communication.

Her level of commitment, however, felt clear. Mother Superior signalled that I was important to her, and this meant a lot to me.

In one parlour session, she asked what I would like to achieve; and I answered that I wanted to be popular. Several days later, talking about behaviour to a group of resident girls, Mother Superior declared something to the effect of, "Anna, whose biggest wish is to be popular, is learning to behave better." I turned beet red and vowed never to tell her anything real again.

She meant well, but lacked the light touch. An example is how she monitored my table manners. Laurier's refectory dining hall was much like Hogwarts school for wizards attended by Harry Potter, with the convent girls eating at long tables facing the nuns' head table. From there, Mother Superior would call out loud reminders to me about taking smaller mouthfuls or breaking my bread before biting into it. She saw me as her special ward, charge and responsibility.

Still, she was the one who reassured me that I was smart and had the very redeemable qualities of openness and honesty. When I left Laurier, Mother Superior said, "This is the opportunity for you to have a fresh start. You can be a good, biddable and studious girl."

I asked if I could change my name, and her reply was, "Why, of course!" That's when I chose to be Anne of Green Gables.

It was this Mother Superior who arranged the psychiatric tests that relieved my young fears of being mentally unstable like my mother. This had been a constant worry since the age of eight. I believe she also passed the results on to my next convent, because I never again sensed that any of the nuns thought I might one day join my mother. I have never forgotten this Mother Superior.

My last convent

St. Charles Academy, in a Winnipeg suburb, was the last of my half dozen residential convents. It was there that I met Sister Augustine, the Mother Superior who may have had the greatest impact on my life.

Early on, she researched my history and found respectable connections on my mother's side of the family: two well-known Manitoba priests, one who later became the Archbishop of St. Boniface.

This established for Mother Superior that I was a good Catholic girl who needed some stability through her adolescence. She was not impressed with the number of convents that preceded hers.

Whenever I was sent to her for discipline, Sister Augustine eyed me with disappointment and sorrow. She always sounded a bit defeated and resigned: "What are we going to do with you?"

Incoherent and distressed by my latest delinquent behaviour, I would burst into tears of agreement. Yes, indeed, what *were* we going to do with me?

I was at least as disappointed as she was. Here I was, in disgrace once more, in spite of all the good intentions instilled in me at our last encounter. Each time, I was terrified that she would finally expel me.

But, no. I remained safe at St. Charles.

Le piano, mon amour

All my convents featured recreation rooms with pianos, where an older girl was always brilliantly playing fast, elaborate pieces such as "Flight of the Bumblebee" or "The Minute Waltz."

Enchanted from the beginning, I pleaded for lessons. Repeatedly, I heard that my father did not think piano lessons were a necessity; and in any case, he lacked the means to pay for them.

It was Sister Augustine who finally made it happen. I don't know how, but piano lessons became a reality when I was 14. Years of frustration and pent-up desire for the instrument drove me to furious daily practice and to beg for more keyboard time. (This gave the nuns a new disciplinary lever: "If you do not behave, you cannot practise.")

After a year, I took and passed the Grade 6 piano exam on strength of my technique and musicality.

But then, instead of the discipline of gradually developing sight reading and other skills, I skipped right to practising and memorizing large, dramatic and showy recital pieces. This might equate to a child being able to recite a literary work by heart without actually learning to read.

I poured my heart and soul into memorizing piano pieces, sinking repressed emotions, sorrows and yearnings into the music. It gave me such a release that the piano became an overwhelming passion. Years later, one former classmate remembered that my playing moved her to tears.

My friends begged me to play for them, and some girls asked me to perform for their parents on visitors' day. It didn't take much coaxing. I loved my role as one of the convent's more promising piano students.

A serious love-hate relationship

Worshipping and adoring my piano teacher, Sister Émile, I strove very hard to impress and please her. I ran into difficulties, however, because of my headstrong ways. Our personalities were incompatible from the beginning.

I was hot-headed, passionate in my opinions and given to creating self-indulgent piano works with overdoses of arpeggios, trills and unnecessary adornments (imagine an unskilled Liberace.)

Sister Émile was distant and mordant, using sarcasm and even occasional contempt to make a point. She had no use for my intensity and what she saw as stubbornness and lack of discipline. My obsession with winning her approval and affection made her uncomfortable, and she never failed to signal quiet disdain. When treated coldly, I sulked.

Walking into the recreation room one day, I heard Sister Émile play hyper-exaggerated series of laughable, frilly arpeggios and chords. To giggles from the girls, she said, "This is how Anne plays."

I muttered "bitch" under my breath. Until then, I had not realized that I even knew the word bitch. It erupted out of me in a moment of deep humiliation and anger that characterized my entire relationship with this nun.

Mother Superior learned about the incident, and I was called to her office. It was the closest I ever came to actually being expelled. Not long afterward, she arranged a piano teacher for me from outside the convent.

Years later, studying psychology, I tried to analyze my traumatic relationship with Sister Émile. I wondered whether trying to win her affections was an attempt to fix a doomed relationship with my own mother who also was cold and withdrawn from me.

Mother Superior was my "go between"

Sister Augustine served as a regular mediator between me and other St. Charles nuns who dealt daily with my misbehaviour (running the halls, cheekiness and insolence in class, rarely turning in homework). I am certain some of them, given the authority, would have expelled me.

One was Sister Geraldine, a fanatically religious person who went on intensely and endlessly about morals. I tried to ignore this teacher. An exception, however, was a lengthy, boring Grade 10 lecture about the perils of dating.

At one point, Sister Geraldine talked about boys trying to seduce girls by petting their arms and progressing elsewhere. Then her arms moved toward her chest. This drew a whisper from the girl sitting beside me, who was usually compliant, responsible and polite. Her quiet comment was, "Does Sister Geraldine know this from personal experience?"

Taking the cue, I raised my hand and asked loudly, "Please, Sister, can you tell us how you learned this information?" All hell broke loose, and she sent me to Mother Superior's office again.

Another time, I hadn't done my usual last-minute cramming for a serious Grade 10 exam in British history.

I panicked and went to see Mother Superior that morning, pleading that I was woefully unprepared and asking whether I might take the test another time. Sister Augustine placed her hand on my forehead, declared my temperature below normal and sent me to bed for the rest of the day.

I thought then that she had taken pity and invented my low temperature; but years later, I learned that my body temperature is ordinarily less than what is considered normal. Whatever the real reason, Mother Superior gave me one day's grace to study.

Boy-crazy girls drove the nuns crazy

Though occasionally insolent and pushing boundaries, I lived in mortal fear of being sent away from the convent. I knew that certain lines were never to be crossed, and was very aware of where they were.

In high school, I learned quickly to show no interest in make-up, fancy hair-dos, rock and roll or boys. The sisters had a no-nonsense attitude about anyone consorting with boys.

I noted that it was often boy-crazy girls who were expelled. Some had been getting wild before coming to the convent, and this was why they were sent there.

The nuns watched these girls carefully. They sported make-up at every opportunity, hiked their skirts above the knees and talked non-stop about weekend outings with boys. It was a bit of a yawn for those of us spending weekends in the convent.

Before the supervising nuns arrived at the Nazareth residence one spring evening, two girls at their bedroom windows struck up a conversation with a pair of boys on motorcycles and agreed to go riding with them.

The nuns arrived as the girls got off the motor bikes and the boys sped away. The sisters couldn't see exactly who the girls were (a positive side of convent uniforms).

Most of the rest of us were unaware of what had happened. Assembling all the Nazareth girls in the common area, the nuns asked sternly who the culprits were. Silence. The Sisters repeated the question several times. Still no response.

Finally, they had us kneel as a group until someone confessed. An hour's wait brought no response, and we continued to kneel. One nun went across the street, apparently to consult Mother Superior, and we were released a short while later.

Someone confessed and someone was expelled. That's how consorting with boys was dealt with.

Sex and the convent

The nuns rarely broached this subject directly. They cautioned us about untrustworthy, lecherous boys and alluded to the actual sexual act as a sanctified, beautiful and sacred act between two married people who were meant to create children for God.

A woman must treat her body as a temple, never cheapening herself before entering into the sacrament of marriage. No one actually talked about how the sexual act was done. To be fair, sex education in the 1950s and 1960s wasn't happening in homes outside the convent either.

In Laurier Convent when I was 12, Mother Superior once had a long, serious talk with me about the sanctity of my body and the importance of guarding my virginity. Again, no nuts-and-bolts were discussed, and I asked no questions. The closest she came was to tell me that there was a difference between boys and girls. Again, no explanation of the difference. I felt very uncomfortable being singled out for this talk in a darkened dormitory.

When it came to marriage itself the woman was deemed the heart and soul of the home, responsible for spiritual guidance and keeping everything together.

On a summer outing, my aunt shocked me with information about periods. Such was the modesty of the older girls that I had never guessed that such a phenomenon existed. When I found out about periods, I couldn't wait to have them and be initiated into the world of "big girls." I didn't attach any shame to having periods, only a sort of "graduation."

I was 17 or so before I discovered that I had an actual vagina. I thought that there were only two orifices "down there," and it was a really long time before I picked up, in small incremental bits of information, where babies came from and how they were created. The whole thing didn't have much appeal for me.

How in the world did I manage to pass?

In mid-20th-century Manitoba, passing or failing a year of high school depended on one's performance on five final departmental exams. They were written and graded by the province's education ministry.

Nothing counted but these tests in June. Other work in the preceding year made no difference. Failing three of the departmental exams meant repeating an entire grade. But you could fail one or two exams and take a make-up "supplemental" in August.

I only passed those exams because I learned how to be an expert crammer. But I always failed math, and always had to rewrite it, putting myself to work in July. I learned necessary formulas by heart, and struggled mentally to wire together concepts such as, "If one number is on top of another, you divide by the bottom one." Every year, I squeaked through the much-feared supplemental math test.

This meant, of course, that I paid attention in classes only at the beginning of the school year. I sped through textbooks that might interest me and spent study periods enjoying books that I chose from the library.

All through high school, I followed that pattern. The copious extra-curricular reading, however, was a good thing. It built an extensive vocabulary, made many required textbooks easy to digest and taught me to write effortlessly.

Cram, Cram, Cram

High school classes at St. Charles convent were small, no grade having more than a dozen students and some with only six.

There was no bullying, and friends were easy to make if one took the time.

I remember with fondness how we came together in mutual terror of the final departmental exams and collaborated to cram for them.

Girls excelling in particular subjects tutored others, and we helped each other through the mysteries of literary analysis and the complexities of calculus. Extensive use was made of *Coles Notes* and reviews of previous years' exams.

Cramming season started in June. We gathered in pairs or small groups, and girls coached girls in classrooms, stairwells and walking around the school.

Our teachers cheered us on with our concentrated efforts, demonstrating that we were all in this together. (Later, I learned that most of the teachers had only completed high school themselves; just a few had met the requirement of the one year's teacher training.)

Mother Superior offers me a deal

At the beginning of Grade 11, I started to feel afraid for my future. Other girls would graduate, return to their families and begin life in the real world. What would I do, with no family and no resources?

Mother Superior must have sensed my worry, or wriggled it out of me in one of my penitent's crying jags in her office.

She made me a proposal. I could stretch Grade 11 and 12 to three years instead of the usual two and pursue more of my piano elective. To pay the extra expenses, I might teach piano to beginners and catechism to the younger children. I accepted eagerly.

My father, who didn't see the use of books or education, had been looking forward for several years to my convent days ending. I know that Mother Superior would have completely run over any timid objections that he might raise to extending my schooling. He never had the stomach to argue with any of the Mother Superiors.

The fog of my final convent year

Thus I lingered in the convent world until my inevitable graduation at 19.

Life in that last year was different. I was surrounded by younger students and couldn't relate to them, because my friends and entire peer group had graduated and moved on with their lives.

I withdrew into a private fog, and my usual daydreaming became more bizarre and less comforting.

For example, I acquired an old steamer trunk in the laundry shed's store room, and brought various articles of clothing to it. I imagined this as my hope chest for the time I would live in a freezing Paris garret, a starving music student. At the same time, I realized that my convent piano studies had started too late for me to earn a living as a pianist.

Another dawning reality was that I had virtually nowhere to go after my graduation. It was out of the question for me to live with my father for reasons which I explain later.

That winter, I daydreamed that a bout of pneumonia might send me floating off this planet in a cloud of consumption, like a character from one of my Victorian novels.

Not having pneumonia, however, I decided to walk barefoot on the frozen Assiniboine River at the bottom of the convent grounds. This, I thought would cause a raging fever. I would go into a sharp decline and conveniently avoid having to deal with an uncaring world.

The daydream did not come true. I did take a barefoot icy river walk one dark Saturday night. But there was no sign of illness the next morning, just some very uncomfortable blisters on the soles of my feet.

Then my focus shifted to becoming a nun. I knew better than to apply to become a postulant with any of the nuns involved in my upbringing, so I won an interview in a different convent.

The Mother Superior there quickly grasped the situation and offered to lend me tuition for Teachers' College. She said that I could reapply to become a nun after teaching a couple of years. I agreed.

Although I had never considered teaching before, it became my ticket into the real world. I could move on to an avenue familiar to me, an institutional, educational setting at Teachers' College.

Graduation excitement, and conflict

The thrill of my graduation from St. Charles was about more than the convent's ceremonies for diplomas and awards. There was also excitement of a different kind.

With their parents' permission, some Grade 12 girls planned a dinner-and-dance celebration at a local hotel. They knew that graduation was the last day of school and the last day also under the nuns' jurisdiction.

Mother Superior could do nothing, although she strenuously opposed parties with boys, especially with liquor consumption and limited adult supervision.

The girls wanted me to join the festivities and were quite persuasive. They would lend me a pretty dress, apply make-up, fix my hair and even find me a boy!

I had mixed feelings, wanting to belong and please my classmates, and feeling also discomfort with being a "party girl."

Mother Superior called me to her office and offered to give me money to go to the movies instead of the graduation night party. I accepted.

Not only was I relieved about not having to attend the party, I also felt caught in a tug of war between the girls and Mother Superior. In the end, I owed allegiance to Mother Superior.

Graduation night was when I saw *Lilies of the Field* and fell in love with actor Sidney Poitier. Later when I saw *To Sir with Love,* I viewed him as a high-minded educated man with morals, and a gentle touch. He was also black and beautiful, a perfect complement to a girl looking to be different.

3

They were my real parents

Feeling the tug of nostalgia

For years after leaving the convent, I dreamt night after night about seeing the nuns again — in a street scene, always a group of them walking in the distance.

I would try to get ahead of the dream nuns, to identify their order from the habits they wore, trying fruitlessly to recognize individuals. The faces would almost be familiar, so I would follow and try to speak to them. Waking always left me with the same sense of longing and loss.

Even now, whenever I see the outside of a convent, I feel a tug of belonging and nostalgia.

I left the convent about the time that nuns as a group faced major changes. The habit as a uniform was on its way out; nuns had different working lives and new opportunities far from convent life, and fewer young women were becoming novices. A way of life was disappearing.

By the time I tried to find the real nuns of my childhood, they were dying off. Now they are almost all gone, but their imprint remains with me.

I have always clung to the nuns who made real efforts with me. I still send cards and letters at Christmas, striving for the right words of gratitude about their attention and even the slightest kindnesses. Over the years, I tried to let them know how I had turned out.

Some responded with news of their lives. One said she was surprised and disappointed that I had given up Catholicism. Others sent copious good wishes and prayers.

Hoping for the nuns' approval and recognition, I came to see how they had been my real parents.

Nuns: authority, beauty and distance

Individual nuns carried authority that was obvious when they entered a room. They could demand immediate silence by sweeping a gathering with their eyes.

Rarely losing control and virtually always impressive, they modulated their voices for effect and their gestures for attention. It was rare for a nun to shout; but if she did, it was with pure intent, purpose and direction.

The nuns managed to look both demure and commanding, with arms folded under the scapular, the sleeveless cloak falling from their shoulders. They were so thoroughly covered that only their hands and face showed. We never saw even a wisp of hair.

For the longest time, because the nuns' faces were essentially all we saw of them, I thought that a woman's face was all that mattered in terms of beauty and appeal. I didn't understand until well into my twenties that a woman's body also figured into her attractiveness, almost as much as her face.

The nuns maintained a delicate but impenetrable distance from us, and we never ventured into the cloistered part of the convent. It was clear this was their inviolate sanctum.

We knew them by the names they received after taking vows. Only rarely did anyone learn what they had been called before becoming nuns. Such privileged information came from families or other sources outside the convent walls. The nuns' real maiden names in the convent carried power and import like that attributed to wizards in Celtic lore.

Poverty, chastity and obedience

The nuns took solemn vows of perpetual poverty, chastity and obedience. I don't think that they struggled very much with the first two vows, which were inherent in the convent's environment.

I remember nuns saying that their most difficult vow was obedience. Bending to it began early. To develop blind and faithful obedience as postulants and novices they were constantly given disagreeable and sometimes fruitless tasks. An example was washing stairs from bottom to top on their knees. I still don't know how they did that. I understand a bit about army life, and learning obedience also being crucial for soldiers in basic training.

When we asked nuns what they missed about secular life, it was invariably not having children; none mentioned missing husbands.

They did reveal that they often prayed for patience and charity, however, and I had the impression that these prayers were to overcome annoyance — with students, one another, or inanimate objects.

I admired all this as I admired saints. But I could not maintain conformity and obedience very long, and consequently, always ended up in Mother Superior's office.

Nuns have a class system

I saw a kind of two-tier class structure in all of my convents: the educated teaching nuns, and others such as the kitchen nuns who were assigned permanently to manual labour.

This followed the Middle Ages pattern of "choir" nuns and "servant" nuns. The latter were lifelong servants because their poor families could not pay adequate dowries to the convent coffers.

Of course in Canada, the difference between paying and non-paying nuns was gradually discontinued, but there were still residual effects, because often Mother Houses had their inception in Europe where these practices originated.

In one of my convents, teaching nuns were called "Mothers" and the others "Sisters;" slightly different costumes (called habits) set them apart. There was also a third class here, working outdoors and wearing a special apron for such "men's work." The third class didn't talk much, so I thought of them as similar to and playing the role of men. The kitchen nuns, however, were generally cheerful and friendly.

Tacit demonstations of differences in status occurred daily in a myriad of ways. Nuns who did not teach were inferior. Thus I grew to believe that education elevates one in life.

Still, I always found the kitchen nuns approachable. Offering to help with their work meant I could be part of a team, which was novel and heart-warming. One summer when I was about 14, and the only girl in the convent, I chose to spend all my time washing pots and pans, and revelling in torrents of appreciation from the kitchen nuns.

A favourite kitchen nun was Sister Audobert (her name that of an obscure saint because each saint's name can be used only once in any order of nuns). She was from Québec, warm, authentic and down to earth. During the regular school year, I rushed to help in the kitchen after dinner because of her kindness and acceptance.

Sister Audobert would roll her eyes at the tiny bits of food left on each and every plate that the dumbwaiter delivered to the kitchen from the upstairs dining room.

Her opposite in every way was a teaching nun, Mother Notre Dame des Étoiles. The simpering daughter of an aristocratic family in France, she annoyed me with her artificial mannerisms, gestures and prissy figures of speech.

Her mission was to teach us to conduct ourselves like ladies. For example, she insisted repeatedly that we leave at least one morsel of food on our plates. This was to show restraint and that we were not little piggies at the trough. It also produced the harvest of wasted food that Sister Audobert found in the dumbwaiter.

The differences between these two nuns help to illustrate the class structure they inhabited.

I was much fonder of Sister Audobert. But my snobbish little heart identified with the educated nuns in terms of what I hoped to become. I did not want to learn to cook and be slotted as somehow inferior.

The class system also played itself out with girls boarding in the convent. Everyone did morning chores for half an hour before school time. If some girls didn't express an interest in academics they were allocated on the chore roster to the kitchens. Other girls perceived to be bookish or school-oriented were sent to clean the music room, the classrooms or the chapel. None of this was talked about, just understood.

Mother Superior and thus the other nuns implied to me that I was of the bookish class. I was never assigned to the kitchen.

It was only years later in a university "Social Stratification" class in Sociology at UBC that I understood the unspoken social dynamics under which I was raised.

Thus when the subject came up after I "entered the world," I would proudly announce that I didn't know how to cook and wasn't the least bit interested.

So many made impressions on me

I met hundreds of nuns in my many years of convent life, and they were more than interchangeable ciphers in identical uniforms. Each was a unique personality in her own right.

Many made impressions on me, but I cannot acknowledge all of them here. This is a sampling of four who were memorable and who influenced me in some way.

Sister Alphius

Not a teacher, Sister Alphius with the Franciscan order of nuns in St. Laurent, worked in the bowels of the convent, making the white cloth shoes worn by all the sisters. She also sometimes supervised the resident girls, and this is how we got to know her.

Sister Alphius would step quietly into a room, shining with palpable calm and serenity. She literally lit the place with a glow of unconditional love for everyone.

Presenting herself most humbly, she was quiet and unassuming, conveying a sense of complete joy in watching over us. There was no chiding or impatience.

That was in Grade 8, when I loved reading the lives of the saints to obtain a grasp on what they were like. Sister Alphius was the only real saint I ever encountered in my convents.

Sister Gabriel

On the first day of Grade 9, our new English teacher encountered a group of shallow girls who preferred pretty-faced nuns. But stocky Sister Gabriel had the gait of a retired football player and, as a classmate recalls today, "the face of a bulldog."

We noticed within minutes that her left arm ended in a stump, with two tiny fingernails where a hand should have been. Shifting in our seats, we tried to stare without being obvious.

Later, there were shuddering stories about the stump lightly brushing us when Sister Gabriel leaned in to see our work. Our shocked reactions, my classmate remembers, seemed to give our teacher a certain satisfaction.

But the singlehanded nun could do almost anything, from wringing a dish-cloth to manipulating a pen as a prop to emphasize a point in a lecture.

Not French Canadian like most of the other nuns, Sister Gabriel was a native English speaker who had converted to Catholicism. She read aloud in English class in a voice conveying the nuanced meanings that we might have missed.

She was our best high school teacher, trying to make us think instead of preaching at us. Her tools were books that opened our narrow little minds to concepts such as euthanasia, acceptance of peoples' differences, forgiving transgressions and even (horrors!) passion and love outside of marriage.

I sneaked away from chapel to read in an obscure corner of the convent and sometimes found Sister Gabriel doing the same thing.

Once, she sighed and said to me, "One day, you could have a whole library of your very own."

Sister Marie de Lorette

A tiny, nervous woman who was terrified of us, Sister Marie de Lorette had bulging blue eyes and pink cheeks that blushed furiously when trying to assert herself in class.

Sister Marie de Lorette seemed a rabbit to me, and we ran roughshod over her — throwing notes across the room, asking silly questions to make her blush, whispering in class, being obviously and deliberately inattentive while lying back in our desks.

We hated ourselves for creating this awful reign of terror, but seemed unable to stop the torture.

Thirty years later, at our reunion, I rushed to Sister Marie de Lorette and apologized profusely for how we girls had disrupted her class. She stopped me and said, "Oh, no, it is I who should apologize for not knowing how to run a classroom. I was so young and incapable."

Her humility and sweetness bowled me over; and I stayed in touch for years, until Sister Marie de Lorette's final days in an extended care hospital.

Sister Veronica

A tall and skeletally-thin nun with a narrow paper-white face crisscrossed by fine wrinkles, Sister Veronica walked as light as air, and her presence was almost otherworldly.

She was the chemistry and sciences teacher. Her lab was a personal domain that felt separate and sepulchral compared to the rest of the convent.

Never needing to raise her voice or assert her authority, Sister Veronica had such a command of the room that no one ever uttered a sound unless asked to.

She addressed us as if we were adults and never spoke down to us, but a quiet, droning monotone voice made her presentations as dry as year-old hardtack.

I assumed that her lectures were accessible to only the most assiduous and attentive students. As soon as I entered the lab, I folded up my tent and went into a deep pseudo sleep. Sister Veronica's lesson for me was that teachers should be lively presenters and invite some interaction.

I never connected with her, not once, and suspect that I wasn't the only student who did not. Later, I learned that she had only half a stomach (that's why she was so thin and white) and was an accomplished though unacknowledged artist.

I meet nuns like no others

At the impressionable age of 13, I met the nuns of the Franciscan Missionaries of Mary, initially spending a school year at their St. Laurent Convent school.

These women strove to literally practise what they preached, to do the real work of the Lord. They wore white habits and seemed to float when moving, as though in touch with God. The Franciscans' piety was striking.

For hours in Chapel, they knelt and meditated before the elaborate gold monstrance, the vessel for the consecrated host that must be worshipped constantly and never be unattended.

The silence and adoration impressed me. I was entranced by the splendid white floor-length light as air veil. Occasionally, I was allowed to wear the same long gorgeous veil and kneel at the altar for an hour of deep devotion.

These nuns influenced me to try to be a better, if not a more saintly, person. I even read *Imitation of Christ* as a devotional book at meals. This was the time in my adolescence when I was at my most pious.

To my child's eyes, these nuns were like no others. They complimented one another and gave supportive accolades to students. They prayed hard to subdue even a whisper of imperfection in themselves. They cultivated humility and love for others.

The Franciscans also served the poor and were true missionaries. At St. Laurent Convent, they worked with Metis and First Nations people in a rural area of Manitoba.

The Franciscan practice of charity

In addition to St. Laurent, I lived with the same order of Franciscan nuns for two summers in Winnipeg. Embedded in what was then an inner city environment on Jarvis Street, their convent was dedicated to charity for the underprivileged.

Every day, the kitchen nuns carefully constructed heavy thick sandwiches for homeless or alcoholic men who came to the door. An ancient nun sat in the vestibule and talked to the men while they ate. I never knew exactly what she said, but it seemed very saintly work.

The convent also operated a day care centre, a summer school and Joan of Arc house "for the protection of young women" which day schooled neighbourhood girls and taught them to sew. This convent also took in refugee women until they could find jobs and apartments of their own.

I learned to embroider pillow cases and dish towels. These were sold door-to-door by pairs of nuns, to raise money in their customary humility, for charitable works.

The convent also had a small, captivating walled courtyard garden. I wandered its miniature paths and prayed intensely to be a better person, in the hidden little grotto there.

4

The mystery of family

Only one set of parents?

For most of my early life, the idea of family confused me, and my experiences with families often made me run back to the convent gratefully. The nuns never talked much about families except in pious terms, and my own family experience was minuscule, having dissolved so early.

When other children were excited about going home, I just took a good book and cocooned in a hidden corner. (For my first convent year, before learning to read, I was simply bored and looked in the toy cupboard for something to do.)

I always looked forward to being alone in the convent with the nuns and my books.

To give me a family experience, the nuns occasionally sent me to visit families for Christmas dinner or short holidays. I often spent the time as a quiet observer, seated primly on a couch and fielding polite questions from people who knew as little about convents as I did about family life.

My life was with the nuns. Their quiet restraint and predictability seemed infinitely better than the chaos I observed on visits to those homes. I sometimes felt sorry for children with only one set of parents, instead of a host of women from whom one could choose models to emulate. I truly felt a tiny bit blessed.

Much later, I realized what a mixed blessing that was.

Lovely mother, terrifying father

When I was about nine, on an overnight "family experience" with non-relatives, the mother asked whether I wanted a snack. I nodded, and she gave me butter and peanut butter on a saltine. I was delighted and made this clear.

So for the next half hour in the kitchen, she carefully fixed and handed me one buttered cracker after another. I enthusiastically went on about having never tasted such a thing and how good it was. For that brief time, I felt a certain connection to her that I never forgot.

I was asleep with the woman's daughter in a curtained alcove off the kitchen when the father came home.

He threw pots and pans and yelled and screamed at his wife — and he even might have hit her. Now as an adult, I understand that the man had been drinking. As a child, I was terrified.

I kept stiff and still in bed and felt the other little girl lying motionless and pressed against the wall. I was afraid her father would rip the curtain away and attack us. That didn't happen, and I went home to the convent the next day with great relief.

Why such an intense attraction?

At my last Franciscan convent, before high school, most of the students came from First Nations families, and I have a strong memory of one fetchingly pretty native girl who was in Grade 1.

Joanie boarded during the week, delivered by an adult every Monday, and was deloused when she arrived. On weekends, she lived with numerous relatives in a shack 13 miles away.

It was considered a mercy that she lived most of the week in our pristine and orderly convent. This was conveyed to me subtly, and I agreed wholeheartedly.

Yet every week, this little girl ran away, walking the 13 miles to her home. I never understood this, and I still think of her to this day.

Was it that she had a loving mother? Did she miss her brothers and sisters? Was this the attraction of a family life that I did not fully understand?

Stranger in a strange land

Being sent off for a family experience put me in strange territory. I might be slightly more comfortable visiting relatives of my own, but even the home life of relatives seemed complicated and problematic.

The difference with relatives was that I wanted to fit in and belong more than I did with strangers.

On a holiday with an aunt's family when I was nine, I noticed that her husband rarely spoke to anyone. He grunted responses to questions and seemed remote, preoccupied and grumpy. This didn't fit in with my idealized idea derived from books. Nancy Drew's father was a friend and mentor.

None of the children addressed my uncle directly; they and my aunt spoke only to one another. The young me thought this might be because he was a farmer with no time for conversation. I decided never to marry a farmer.

In my late teens, with my maternal great uncle's family, I admired the children's musical abilities and their apparent willingness to do chores without being asked. This family was peaceful, but also lived with an uncommunicative, intimidating and remote father.

I really wanted to belong to such a cultured, progressive and educated clan, but my convent upbringing had somehow affected my ability to work as part of a team without specified rules. I always felt like an outsider looking in.

From one family visit to another, the rules always varied: it was never clear exactly what they were. I felt sorry for kids who lived permanently in foster care where they were never really part of the family. Often, I felt out of sync, wrong footed and unable to figure out where I went amiss. When uncomfortable silences occurred, I wondered whether they were caused by subtle or gross missteps of mine: inappropriate questions, remarks, actions or inaction.

Having said that, however, there was a two-week summer holiday on a farm when, as a teen, I was able to help my uncle's family bale hay, from morning till night. I stood on the hay rick and, as part of the team, grabbed and swung 80-pound bales of hay to my cousin who then swung them into place further back on the rick.

When I sat at meals with my cousins, I felt for the first time that I really had a place. Those two weeks were the highlight of my family experiences.

However, I had a better understanding of my place in the convent. I "belonged to the nuns," and, in a weird way, had made them my family.

Changing my mind about families

Only much later, as an adult, did I understand some of what I had missed by not having a full-time, loving mother. Never actually seeing a parent love a child, I didn't think then that I was missing much.

Loving parents were part of the make-believe world of books. As a child, I didn't think such people existed.

Of course, I did observe some parents giving their convent daughters candy and care packages and money to buy treats for afternoon snacks. But I also noticed that other girls with families never received chocolates and spending money. I wasn't the only one.

I noticed, too, that some girls with families carried themselves with a certain unshakable self-confidence. They did not feel the need to show off or call attention to themselves. They quietly did their homework and tasks, and were naturally obedient and willing to follow the rules. I wondered if this was due to belonging to a family.

In my world, so many things were beyond control — being pretty, having naturally curly hair or coming from a real family.

5

My own lost family

Whatever Daddy says about life, do the opposite

My relationship with my father, Thomas St. Onge, was a tragic one, for both of us. I don't know if we were close when I was a toddler, but I started to feel deeply ashamed of him when I was out of the family and into convent life.

I felt my father's appearance reflected poorly on me, and diminished my worth in other people's eyes.

He became a father late in life, so I always knew him as an old man — with very broken English, only one front tooth and a big belly. My father wore coke-bottle glasses and baggy, unwashed, depression-era overalls. Today, If I saw him in the street, he would look like a homeless person.

In his rural setting, my father came off as a "Tom from the bush." He looked generally shabby and always drove a horse and buggy. Although legally blind, he managed in his log cabin and outdoors with his horses.

I was a harsh critic and compared him very unfavourably with other fathers who visited the convent in cars or trucks, looked presentable and had tidy wives.

Alone with me, my father delivered straightforward pronouncements in an intense, loud voice:

"Money don' grow on trees, you know. You cost me a lotta money."

"What that school gonna get you anyway. Don't teach you to cook... nobody gonna marry you!"

"You read too many books, gonna make you crazy like your mudder."

"You done finish Grade 5. Now you gonna get a job... help on a farm. get yourself married."

"What de piano gonna get you? Cost lotta money, not gonna get you a husband."

"Too much religion make you sick like too much jam."

"You don't seem to know dis, but you gotta learn in life that you gotta eat shit."

My father hadn't stepped out of the old habitant world of rural Québec where he was born in 1903, and possibly because of failing eyesight hadn't gone beyond Grade 3. He didn't believe in education, didn't trust books, disliked religion — scoffed at refinements like sheets, cupboards that weren't apple crates and other trappings of so-called civilized living.

Maybe once or twice a year, he visited me in the convent, when he could hitch a ride with someone else traveling such a formidable distance.

My father was very much out of his element visiting the convent. Around the nuns, he shuffled uncomfortably into the room, twirled his cap in his hands, looked down at his feet and responded to questions in monosyllabic mumbles. Helpless really, he acquiesced to any of Mother Superior's suggestions. Thankfully, she was the one who kept me in school.

Dreading these visits, I gave him the civil required greeting and kiss, and acted the "polite little girl with her daddy." I hoped and prayed that he wouldn't be seen by anyone and would hurry back to his home in the bush.

If this is love, it's very faint

Once or twice, my father took me to a local café where there were booths that I liked, and still like, because of their privacy. As a kid with my dad, they were wonderful hiding places, where I was offered milk shakes.

When I was about nine, he and I sat in a booth, and I felt warmth coming from my father. I remember thinking this might be love. I decided, "If this is love, it's very faint, barely detectable." I wasn't certain, but had read about love and thought this warmth radiating from him might be what the books talked about.

Sometimes, my father looked at me in wonder and disbelief, as if I was amazing. But I didn't value this because I was unable to see beyond his flaws. Now I know that my father loved me. And I, too, loved him, but didn't know it at the time.

I called him "Daddy" until he died. I never moved it to "Dad."

Learning what *not* to do

I recognize my love for my father today, but feelings of shame dominated the picture when I was young. How did I treat him? Mostly with rejection, scorn and contempt.

I made derogatory mental notes about my father: his failure to keep a clean cabin and his cautionary pronouncements on life. I made choices that were the exact opposite:

Read bigger books, opt for education and stay in school as long as possible.

Avoid the bush and marriage to a farmer

Keep a tidy home, play the piano, get classy, become refined.

At all costs, don't go home to live with him.

As an adult, and long after my father had died, I could see him objectively and recognize at last the qualities I had ignored as a child.

He never drank, and never took up with poor single women, although a few offered their company. An honest, straightforward man, my father always conscientiously paid his bills on time. Throughout the depression, he rode the rails for a time, and slept in barns and earned a pittance as a hired man on other people's farms.

My father was truly a man of a distant age, thrust into a future he didn't understand and with which he never caught up.

A mental picture of home, and the stark reality

I spent two summers with my father in his cabin by Lake Spence, and about three Christmases there with him and my brother, Léon.

Before those visits, when my father first told me about the cabin, I had pictured scenes from the book *Heidi* which I had read when I was about nine. I imagined him as the book's elderly man, with a rustic cabin on a mountain in idyllic surroundings of nature and trees.

I was keen to be Heidi and help take care of the cabin — the good daughter of the house. In my mind's eye, I would sweep the wooden floor with a straw broom and sleep in the loft on a sweet-smelling bed of hay. We would eat black bread and cheese, washed down with milk or fresh lake water. In a tidy apron, I would use a strong brush to scrub the rustic table, spread a red-and-white check tablecloth on it, and set out our simple meal.

I was ten in the summer of my first visit. When my father opened the door to his home, I just stood there, shocked.

The cabin was small and made of rough logs. Lining a side wall were two dirty mattresses covered by rough horse blankets. Cupboards on another wall were apple crates. A table held a coal oil lamp and a container of strawberry jam covered by flies. Lined with years of encrusted dirt, a basin sat on a sideboard. Lying beside a bucket was a grimy grey dishcloth, dry and twisted into rigour mortis because the mineralized lake water hardened rags into the shapes they took when wet.

Near the doorway stood a small stove used for heat and cooking. Nearby was a stack of firewood and, on the other side of that, an abandoned, corroded wood stove with four ancient flatirons rusting on its surface.

There were no cleaning supplies like those in the convent, like Old Dutch scouring powder, dish detergent, steel wool, brushes, any useable towels or cloths.

I learned after a while that mice or rats climbed from the swampy crawl space under the cabin floor to forage for leftover sandwiches.

After one visit to the nearby lake, I decided to make the lake my home and enter the cabin as little as possible.

I became an avid swimmer, totally at one with the lake. I admired the boulders surrounding the lake and became fleet-footed, leaping and hopping from one boulder to another for what seemed like miles, never slipping or a setting a foot wrong.

I spent hours sitting on a special large rock, talking, singing and making up poetry for the lake. I treated the lake like a real person. It was vast, receptive, sparkling and soothing — a great protective spirit of water and light.

My father meets his grown-up daughter

In the summer of my last year at a convent school, I received a note scribbled on a shred of paper ripped off the corner of a page: "I'm sick, come home for a visit."

Either my father had written the note or gotten someone else to. It couldn't have been my brother. By then, 21 years old, Léon was living in Alberta. At 19, I was independent and found a ride to my father's new home in Rorketon, a little south of his home village.

He had received an inheritance from an older brother and bought a modest bungalow just outside Rorketon.

Sitting on rough pilings, the house had running water, electricity, a kitchen sink with cold running water and an electric fry pan that handled all the cooking needs. Water could be boiled on the old cabin's box wood stove that stood near the counter. There were a table and chairs, and an armless couch in the living room that could do double duty as a make-shift bed. My father had his own bedroom, and it actually had a bed and dresser. There was an outhouse in the back yard.

I had spent a previous Christmas here with my father and brother, but I had never returned because there was no nearby lake where I could take comfort.

My father was exceedingly proud of how this elaborate living space compared with the old cabin in the woods. I was somewhat older and more critical of the new house. To me, it spelled poverty and squalor, and seemed even more uninviting than the shack in the bush where my father had lived before. There were unwashed dishes on the counter, bare mattresses and a bucket for urine.

An adult now, I was able to get my father to pay for cleaning materials, and I scrubbed the house from top to bottom. I also bought sheets for the bed.

He complained about being unable to find anything, and seemed somehow awkward about the new bedding. But I could tell that my father was impressed with his grown-up, bustling take-charge girl.

The best lie I ever told

He and I arranged a ride to take me to the city and the Teachers' College where I would be in residence. An order of nuns had loaned me the tuition money, and I had acquired a job in the cafeteria to help with my living expenses.

While we sat awkwardly waiting for the ride, my father asked, "Why didn't you never like me?"

I froze. This conversation was on a level we had never reached before. Then I started to cry and just couldn't stop the tears.

Finally, I got a grip and told him the best lie I've ever told anyone in my life. "It's because you always preferred my brother to me. You kept him at home, and you sent me away."

My father also started to cry, and there we were… in tears together.

He protested over and over that I was wrong, and that he had always cared about me as much as my brother.

There was a sense of the finality of this parting. We both knew I wouldn't be back, that this house was not my home.

I offered my father the best thing I owned, a portable alarm clock that the nuns had given me for my graduation. He gave me $80, a large sum in 1964. We cried some more, and then the ride came.

The last I ever saw of my father, he was standing awkwardly in the yard as the car pulled away.

He died suddenly from a heart attack the following spring, when I was in Teachers' College. I was 20 years old.

The story of my mother

Growing up, I had a sense that my mother, Thérèse St. Onge, didn't love me as much as my father did. A major reason was that she, too, was raised without the care of a mother and couldn't be an affectionate mother herself.

My maternal grandmother was a teacher before she married, and fell victim to post-partum psychosis and schizophrenia. This created a situation in which she was unable to take care of her ten living children. My grandmother could be found in one of three places: withdrawn in her bedroom, at the hospital having another child, or living in Brandon Mental Hospital.

A fire had destroyed the family farm. Her husband, now unable to farm, was often away from home, working as an itinerant peddler or hired man in the district, while the oldest boy hunted rabbits to feed the other children. Soon they were all dispersed throughout the extended family, becoming helpers and servant girls when they were old enough.

The children had such difficult lives that three of them also became mentally ill and were in Brandon Mental Hospital and other hospitals until their deaths. For quite some time, my grandmother lived in that hospital with three of her grown children. She remained aloof from them, however, shut away in her own world.

As an elderly woman, herself in a home for the mentally ill, my mother spoke once about my grandmother: "I was the one who missed my mother the most. I was always knocking on her door asking for her."

My mother was eleven years old when my grandmother went into Brandon Mental Hospital for good. This was after the birth of her last child, and she remained there for 65 years, dying at nearly 100 years of age.

She found solace in religion

When my mother was young, she attended school beyond my father's third grade level, but no one knows how far. My mother was described as musical and artistic, with a flair and facility for drawing and for singing, dancing and sewing. She could create garments from any material and fashioned her own wedding dress during World War II.

She found great solace in Catholicism, becoming more and more devout through her teens and into her twenties. For a time, she worked for an extremely devout uncle who taught her about the rigours of self abnegation and mortification of the flesh, not uncommon Catholic practices at that time. One of her cousins admired how my mother spent long periods of time in prayer, kneeling on her hands.

She applied to be a nun but wasn't accepted, possibly because of the mental illness in her family. At about the same time, she began to dress as a nun as she worked for relatives in the village. This seemed strange even in that devout environment.

Hard times after marrying

In 1941, my mother met my father, Thomas, then working as a hired man in the district. My mother was trying so hard to be a saint that I wonder now if she was attracted by his last name: St. Onge. They married that December when she was 27 and he was 38. It was done quickly when he was just starting to surmise that there might be something amiss with his fiancée.

My father took her to the bush to live pioneer-style, without any amenities and four miles from any neighbours. It was a sparsely-populated impoverished countryside, alkali-soaked land where hay was the only crop that could be grown.

That winter my father pointed to a large tract of land and announced that my mother needed to build a garden there in the spring. She seemed able to deal with the difficult life after the birth of her first child, eleven months after the marriage. Two years later, I was born.

The poverty, hardship and wartime conditions wore her down. My mother was in grave psychological difficulty and experienced post-partum psychosis as her mother once had. Three months after I was born, she was taken to Brandon Mental Hospital for a lengthy stay.

My two-year-old brother was placed with a family in the village, and I was taken to a paternal aunt in Laurier, a village 46 miles away. My mother returned to the family cabin for Christmas, and somehow could just manage for the next four years.

Then the family home burned down. My father, brother and neighbours were sawing wood in the yard while my mother made bread inside. She joined them in the yard, and everyone noticed that the cabin was on fire.

My mother apparently raced to break a window, climb inside and rescue me — a laughing baby jumping up and down in her crib and crowing at the flames.

My reaction was typical. I was a child who seemed to be in perpetual motion. My father told me that before the house burned down, he constantly had to nail together the crib because I kept shaking the bars loose.

Looking back, the story of the fire shows me that, although unable to demonstrate affection, my mother cared.

The fog of a disturbed mind

No doubt my mother loved me, but her love never reached me through the fog of her disturbed mind.

My mother expanded her religious devotions, and her behaviour became increasingly disturbing. For instance, she tied me to chairs or stalls in the barn because I was an overactive child. The knots were so tight that the neighbours sometimes had to help undo them.

Another memory is of kneeling with my arms tied in front of me with string, locked in the position of prayer. With some effort, I squeezed my arms together and wriggled out.

I steeled myself against her delusions which seemed to focus on me. This was probably because of her illness after my birth and our early separation. I know that our connection was disrupted because I never consciously missed her. Instead, I constructed an idealized version of a Greek-goddess-like figure. I pretended this was my real mother: beautiful, distant and unattainable.

I didn't seek to be near my mother or experience any loss when she left for Bandon Mental Hospital. As time went on, I only felt emptiness where her presence might have been. What might have been a strong affectionate bond had long been broken.

Later in St. Rose convent, when I was about nine years old, I started writing to my mother. They were polite formal, letters guided by the nuns on Sunday mornings after breakfast, the official letter-writing time.

She wrote back, but the sentences jumped incomprehensibly from one topic to another, and I couldn't decipher them. Sometimes, she wrote disturbing messages, for instance about killing me if I didn't behave. I showed the nuns one of these letters, and all communication stopped for many years.

I was 14 years old the first time I saw her in Brandon Mental Hospital, where my Aunt Toni had taken me for a visit. My mother recognized me, insisted that I was much younger than my actual age, and couldn't be convinced otherwise. She was very matter of fact, not excited to see me not even surprised. I just felt awkward and strained. The visit lasted half an hour, and I was relieved to leave, especially after she took a moral tone and told me not to cheat in school.

I was 18 the next time I saw my mother. At another aunt's place, with many people around, we just exchanged a light greeting. There was no conversation, just awkwardness again.

My father died when I was 20, and Léon and I went to Brandon Mental Hospital to see if we should take my mother to the funeral. But she was so cavalier and off-handed about the death of her husband that I took it upon myself to decide against taking her.

My mother's final years

I didn't see my mother again until the 1980s when my brother brought her from Manitoba to Riverview Mental Hospital in British Columbia. By then, both Léon and I were living in BC.

I visited my mother at Riverview on a number of occasions, and something she said chilled me to the bone: "You'll be coming here to join me soon." That touched an old chord. I hadn't realized that the old ghost of insanity could still affect me. I finally gave up the fear at about 50 years of age. That's when I realized that I probably would get dementia before I ever got schizophrenia.

(Later, I came to understand that my mother was lobotomized and subjected to numerous electric shock treatments in her early days at Brandon Mental Hospital. Recently, it has also come to light that seriously unethical experiments were conducted on patients when my relatives were at that hospital.)

When I moved to the Lower Mainland from northern BC, my mother was for the first time at a reasonable distance for me to visit. I saw her when I could at Delta Lodge in Ladner, where she had been transferred from Riverview. The lodge was a facility for the geriatric mentally ill, my mother's last home.

Still unable to maintain a conversation, she would speak non-stop, going off on a multitude of tangents. I had difficulty with these visits at first, but over time I learned to choose a single topic like "friends." For example I kept drawing back to the topic with questions such as "Did you have good friends when you were a child? Who are your friends here?" (She had no close friends and identified more with staff than with the other residents.)

She often started on a topic, but within seconds changed direction, inserting insights about her past. Like shards of jeweled glass, these gave me glimpses such as: "My dear father was the most gentle man. He never raised his voice."

My mother and I found we could sing old French songs together that I had learned in the convent. She remained rooted in the 1930s in her beliefs and attitudes, not believing that I had graduated because only men could do that. She found "negroes" shocking to see, and believed brides likely pregnant.

Eventually, my mother suffered a hemorrhagic stroke and was unable to speak or swallow for the last month of her life. This was in Delta General Hospital, where I was finally able to speak to her.

I told my mother what a gifted seamstress and artist she had been, how she had worked so hard in her youth for other people. Her eyes followed me closely as I sang French songs to her, and I recited her familiar Catholic prayers. I felt at peace with her at last in those moments of connection.

She died quietly one early morning at the age of 85. I mourned the mother and daughter that we might have been if we had known each other.

Where is my brother?

As far back as I can remember, even as a toddler and preschooler, I followed my brother and sought his attention. But Léon was a busy boy.

He was two years older, and focused on his slingshots, bows and arrows, forts, and wood carving. Much later, I came to understand that this fit a general pattern. In many families, younger sisters seek the notice and regard of their older brothers.

Léon spent his childhood years in the village where we were born and was raised in that depressed region, with its forests, the outdoors and fishing. He has lived the country life ever since.

After our mother left, Léon was placed in five or six foster homes in the area. When he was about 12-years-old, my father took him home to his cabin.

Léon was a quiet boy who avidly constructed small tools, snares, fishing rods, snowshoes, and various weapons for surviving in the woods. As a pre-teen, he was comfortable using a .22 calibre rifle to practice on assorted targets.

He had a talent for drawing, sketching and painting animals and nature. He had little interest in attending school which was a great distance from the cabin.

Early on, Léon bonded with our mother and developed a strong sense of wanting to belong and be in a family. He befriended a few boys in the district and, whenever he could, stayed with their large families for several days at a time, so he wasn't always at home with his dad. Over time, he adopted the Seventh Day Adventist beliefs of one family and attended their religious summer camps.

Memorable times together

From the age of four, I spent a total of only about eleven sporadic weeks with Léon, through a couple of summers and three Christmas holidays. I worked hard for his attention, playing his games with him and volunteering to be his assistant, dare taker, or whatever it took to share Léon's company.

Mostly we swam in the lake, inventing various diving games, and trying to stay underwater longer and longer. On shore, we used rushes to build a little hideaway in the bushes, and we boulder-jumped like goats from rock to rock. I never tired of this, as we saw little of one another outside those holiday visits.

The most memorable times with Léon were the summers when I was ten and eleven. He came and went for several days at a time.

When at the cabin, he occupied himself with projects like building a little model ship that fell on its side in the lake and a belt to carry assorted survival devices. I remember one was a torch-like apparatus that could be lighted for starting fires. He also concentrated on creating better and better sling-shots to hit moving targets.

In the second summer, Léon taught me to ride his bike. This took a bit of work as it was a boy's bike and the trails were bumpy and overgrown.

We never fought as children because I was eager to be his follower and because we never got to know each other well enough to generate a quarrel.

When I became an adult, I moved on. We grew farther and farther apart because our worlds were very different. Eventually, in our sixties, we came together again and started getting to know one another as adults.

Why did we grow apart?

As children, my brother and I were raised in totally different environments, even speaking in slightly different accents. Our lives took different paths.

Léon valued his new religion; I dropped mine. He earned his living as a tree faller; I became a tree hugger. He was rurally oriented; I was essentially a city girl. He liked hunting and fishing; I couldn't stand the thought of an animal suffering.

Before agreeing to go to a movie now, I still ask if it shows animals being hurt. He lives a traditional blue-collar lifestyle, with the wife in the kitchen and the man working outside. I really fought those stereotypes and took pride in studious pursuits instead of cooking.

Still, from what I remember and have been told, I have come to understand that Léon was a docile boy. Here is an example of how compliant he was. A foster parent once told Léon to keep still while she traced his feet on a sheet of paper before ordering a pair of shoes from a catalogue. She was called away and came back to find him still standing there a long time later (hours they said, but I think that's an exaggeration).

In the end, Léon grew into a talkative adult with ideas about everything in his life. I wanted to converse as equals, to have Léon show curiosity about my life, my ideas, my values, as much as I did about his.

We didn't meet often as adults. Each time, I left feeling upset, angry, frustrated and as if I didn't matter to him. Eventually, we both became angry and impatient with each other and stopped communicating.

Building a good relationship

In 2011, Léon's home in central BC burned down, and he and his wife, Evelyn, were admitted to a hospital burn unit near my home in Vancouver. I went to visit them, but couldn't continue. I had a very bad cold, and the risk of infection was too great. Just turning 40, Leon's youngest son, Raymond, an affable, loving and steady man stayed at my apartment and mediated between Léon and me.

During these hospital visits, Raymond told Léon what a wonderful person I was. Then he would see me and describe all my brother's myriad quixotic talents. Raymond also impressed on me that everyone experienced Léon's communication style essentially as I did, and that I shouldn't take it as lack of interest in me personally. My brother was like that with everyone.

Then the hospital released my brother and Evelyn, and they recuperated at my place for week before going home. Léon and I buried the hatchet and, slowly and tentatively, developed a good relationship. He and I will always have some difficulty understanding each other's worlds, but we continue to try.

6

What became of Anna

The convent girl stereotype

There is a stereotype, sometimes true, that convent girls go wild after they leave the nuns' strict upbringing. I was no exception.

I was 20 and attending Teachers' College in Manitoba when my father died. My brother, Léon, wasn't nearby, but in Alberta. So having always felt alone in the world, I realized rapidly then that I would have to fend for myself.

I didn't identify it as such, but I left the convent with a huge need for love. I also felt mixed up about a lot of things, and uncertain about my attachment to the nuns' teachings.

Not that interested in boys, but worried about being abnormal, I decided at the age of 22 to find out where I was with all of this. I made a conscious decision to have sex.

I picked an educated young man with an exotic Caribbean accent who reminded me of my heroes, Sydney Poitier and Harry Belafonte. I didn't learn much about myself from my West Indies boyfriend, except that I was uncertain about what men should be like, and that I was unready for a lifetime commitment.

Then I accidentally became pregnant with this boyfriend's child. At 23, I gave birth to a stunningly lovely baby girl, Mara. Before she was born, I had thought of giving her up for adoption. Afterward, I fell head-over-heels in love with her and decided that I would live in a ditch rather than give up my baby.

Mara's father was a responsible man who asked me to marry him, saying that he had made his bed and "now must lie in it." I declined his proposal.

Instead of marriage, I moved to Vancouver, a single mother with a bi-racial baby.

Different and non-conformist

In Vancouver, I adapted the 1960's church teachings that "God is Love" to the free-wheeling lifestyle of the hippy movement.

This suited me immensely, and it met my need to be different and non-conformist. Always choosing the path less travelled, I lived in a commune, was a lighthouse keeper, studied at university and for four years worked as a social worker in an isolated First Nations' village.

I also went through several relationships and jobs, learning by a process of elimination what I didn't want or couldn't manage.

I tried hard to make relationships work with one man after another. I had no clue about the kind of investment that an egalitarian relationship entailed, but I wouldn't settle for anything else.

My upbringing had been a strange mixture of submission, adoration, obedience and rebellion. Out of the convent, I was shocked to find out that the world actually believed men to be superior to women. I didn't know how to deal with this.

Going through a series of relationships, I both rebelled and capitulated, gave up my beliefs, put my partner on a pedestal and tried to adopt all of his beliefs. This made me crashingly dependent, insecure and adoring.

I worked on relationships the way one might do homework. It was all about changing myself in order to be a better partner, or trying to change my partner to make him a better man. All the while, I kept fighting both my partners and myself to retain independence.

I yo-yoed back and forth between being slavish and demanding, insecure and overly confident. I didn't understand men, and they certainly didn't understand me.

Education, career, partnership

Through all of that, I saw the need to create a strong base for my daughter and me. One way was trying to make relationships work. As time went on, however, it became clear that I might not be successful in this. I decided to get a good education and finally become independent.

I discovered my real vocation by the age of 30. Psychology had deeply intrigued me since my teens, and I sought books on Freud and others like him, anything I could find about mental illness. Of special interest was learning how to avoid becoming mentally ill myself and leading a well-adjusted life.

I found out who I really was; a person comfortable helping others to survive trauma and difficulty, and to be proactive in reshaping their lives. I was good at assisting people in developing coping skills, and I discovered that my specialty was facilitating counselling groups, as well as providing therapy to individuals. Later, I also found that I really enjoyed teaching adult college students.

Interestingly, I also learned through my studies that children raised in institutions often have trouble maintaining healthy relationships and keeping their families together.

Over the years, I applied myself assiduously to serious study — through night school, correspondence courses and some full-time winter sessions at UBC. After 25 years of dedicated work, I earned two bachelor's degrees and two master's degrees in social work and counselling.

After university, my career involved therapist positions in mental health centres, part-time college teaching and working with sex offenders. I also worked with men who were abusive in their relationships with women.

By my early 50s, I understood enough about relationships to form a long-term partnership with a man who, like myself, has non-conformist ideas and is principled, bookish, conversational, loyal and dependable.

We live in separate apartments in the same building, providing support and companionship to one another. This gives us the independence both of us crave. This 20-year relationship is a record and a satisfying achievement for each of us.

How did my convent years affect me?

Many of the coping skills I had learned were acquired as a convent girl.

There is no way to know what my life would have been like without those convent years. But indications are that I wouldn't have thrived in my family of origin, or done well in that village where children of the poorer families rarely went far in school. Certainly, I wouldn't have been very happy in foster care.

Luckily, I wasn't placed in a real orphanage with other children who had no families. Being overlooked in that setting would have damaged me. I (now) recognize that some girls suffered even worse mistreatment and neglect in some convent schools across the world.

Convent life varied a great deal in different convents — depending on the era, the nuns' orders, the culture in individual convents, and the nuns' level of education. For instance, my experience was dramatically different from the horrific conditions suffered by young women incarcerated in the Magdalene Laundry institutions of Ireland.

I was lucky to be raised in convents where corporal punishment was rarely used. During the 1960s, the idea of "God is love" was starting to replace the "God will punish you" theology.

But it's important to note that being raised in most convents did mean emotional neglect and a serious lack of understanding about how each child needs positive individual recognition, attention, affection and caressing.

Especially at St. Charles Convent, sick or injured children were left unattended in the young children's dormitory and received only food and minimal care. Rarely were children taken to a doctor, and serious conditions were sometimes ignored or treated lightly. Fortunately, during my time, children were sent home before any fatalities occurred.

Structure, focus and guilt

From the start, what saved me was the feeling that I had a unique status in the convent. I was an insider who actually belonged to the nuns. This was beyond the experience of other convent girls, and certainly of children placed with relatives or in foster care.

I was impressed early with convent architecture, which made convents seem more like castles than institutional settings. I knew that I was fortunate to be there, and never felt exiled from a loving home. In fact, I felt saved.

The convent led me to create personal, internal systems and rules for myself. I came to recognize that in order to function well, I must always make myself accountable to achieve what I want. From childhood to the present, this has been a pattern that works for me. So choosing employment with a government organization where I could carve a unique niche allowed me to thrive.

I perceived the nuns as always focused on striving to be better people. They did this with self-imposed guilt and self-examination through prayer and confession.

For me, guilt over every little transgression has remained. In the Catholic church, every action, every thought, every intention is up for examination and judgment. Each has a category, a venial sin or a mortal sin. It becomes difficult to stop second-guessing oneself at every step. This is still something I struggle with today.

Resetting my moral compass

Reading what other women have written about their convent experiences, I found that most battled guilt for the rest of their lives. (Examples are in *Convent Girls,* interviews collected and compiled by Jane Tolerton, and in writing by convent girls, edited by Jackie Bennett and Rosemary Forgan.)

Their assessments of convent experience cover a broad spectrum, from bitterness, anger and rage to a joyful recounting of idealized experiences. Many left Catholicism altogether, although a good proportion of convent girls remained staunch practicing Catholics.

From my 20s, I consciously tried to reinvent my entire moral, social, and emotional structure. I threw out many Catholic teachings.

I finally found a sound footing after a period of indifference to dogmatic issues of right and wrong. Gradually, I fixed my moral compass on ideas that I could trust and believe in — such as the golden rule, self-awareness, empathy, and philosophies that don't impose strict doctrines.

From convent girl to mother

I was bowled over by the intensity of my feelings for my newborn daughter, Mara. Taking the long view now, I see how the limitations resulting from my upbringing affected her.

I raised Mara much as Mother Superior raised me — keeping a distance, fretting over her, always trying to expose her to my own beliefs about what she needed.

Mother Superior especially, and the other nuns, concentrated on my moral and character development, mostly around submission, good behaviour and obedience. By example and in lectures, they tried in every way to implant correct thinking and respectful actions and attitudes. Some attention was paid to less spiritual needs like prescription glasses and replacing worn shoes. To a much lesser degree, this also applied to my education.

I didn't find my convent upbringing problematic. As a child, I saw nothing wrong with what the nuns did, believing that they were virtually perfect and that my troubles were of my own making. This left me unprepared for my later role of a good mother.

Growing older, I looked for guidance in textbooks. My psychology courses mainly dealt with behaviourist approaches to childrearing — reinforcement, consequences, extinguishment and enrichment. This was the emphasis, along with providing lots of different stimulating experiences to build the child's IQ.

I also really focused on self-esteem. I wanted to give Mara a strong sense of independence, and help her explore and take risks to overcome fear and dependency. She was complimented profusely on her appearance, her independence and her accomplishments.

The goals were to make her as strong as possible, with high self-regard, able to deal with hardship, fend for herself, stand on her own and have a love of books and reading. Mara developed all these attributes in spades.

My principal approach consisted of teaching, advising and lecturing. I see now that this instructional mode was an exact reenactment of the way the nuns always occupied my personal time.

What Mara really needed, however, was to be showered with love, affection, attention and devotion. I didn't have a clue how to do that. In the 1950s and 1960s, when I was raised, little was said about attachment theory, bonding, and even breast feeding — certainly not by the nuns.

But miracle of miracles, that generational chain has been broken. My daughter is the most affectionate, devoted, attentive and demonstrative mother I've ever seen.

Mara has created a strong, stable family unit in a long-term marriage. At the same time, she takes good care of her children, as well as two special-needs adults who live with the family. Those responsibilities haven't kept her from fashioning a satisfying career, teaching educators and others about emotional self-regulation for children.

I am proud of my daughter, and grateful for the opportunity to be an affectionate, attentive, loving grandparent to her children. This second chance is rarely given to those in my situation.

Generating another family for myself

The convent warped my idea of family life; in my 20s most of my hippy friends were estranged from their families. This reinforced my weird ideas of what families are all about.

I didn't get much exposure to healthy families. My friends expressed their sorrow to me about being rejected by one or both of their parents. Most of the time I was thankful I had no parents or family.

Although I wasn't very interested in close friendships in the convent, my adult friends became principal sources of support and enjoyment. I had a sense that I needed to reach out to others, without waiting to be chosen by those I liked. I couldn't believe that they would choose me on their own anyway.

They had their own families, and I saw it as my job to create and maintain ongoing connections in life.

My idea was to generate family in a close coterie of chosen friends. Many people with real families could always gravitate back to home, hearth and kin. But I rounded up my friends for tête-a-têtes, dinners, parties, holidays and other events.

I became known as the sheepherder, the gatherer; and my home was Grand Central Station. I kept friends close through the years with visits, letters, cards and phone calls. I invested time and love in people with whom I had a history, including ex-boy friends.

Writing this book has helped me understand the choices I made in my life. Most of all, it has alleviated the sense I had of girl Anna being the problem child. So many institutionalized children in the literature struggled harder and longer than I did, and many had more difficult times.

I now only feel deep gratitude for the kindnesses shown to me by strangers. Giving me all they could, they enabled me to lead a fulfilling, happy and contributing life. Thank you.

Acknowledgements

I owe thanks to so many people who helped me to tell this story.

First, I am grateful to those who took time to read early versions of some vignettes and give thoughtful feedback: my high school friend, Jeannette St. Pierre, whose lively family I remember so well; Clementine Lagimodière who weathered Laurier Convent with me; and Yvonne Verhaeghe whose own memories confirmed my recollection of St. Charles experiences.

Special thanks go to Germaine Verhaeghe for her encouragement, validation and support of my efforts to paint a true picture of the convent years we shared. She gave me immeasurable support as I struggled with details of our common experiences, and her enthusiasm helped me through some of the rougher parts of my memories.

Others who didn't grow up in convents also gave me useful feedback and spurred me on: Conrad Hadland, Brinsley Stewart, Judy Taylor-Atkinson, Michele Ley, Alan Wood, Bob Forrest and Leon and Angie Van Noorden.

John Thompson deserves special recognition for his careful scrutiny and analysis of the manuscript. Gay Jackson edited the book. Both made very helpful suggestions!

Thanks also go to Linda Coe for her heartfelt response to my story and her hard work to give the book a solid graphic foundation.

Most of all I thank my dear partner, Jerry, for the hundreds of hours he gave to put my story book into a readable form. His support and comfort helped me through the more arduous days of writing and rewriting this work.

Anna St. Onge
Vancouver, BC • November 2016

Made in the USA
San Bernardino, CA
16 February 2017